"Every now and then a clear voice rises from the ashes of America's Fireground and Dan Lliteras is one of these. A former fire fighter, Lliteras knows the voice of urgency and crisis, elements that make you feel you are there with the characters in his stories. He is a writer to watch, and to read."

—Dennis Smith, author of *Report from Engine Co. 82*

"I read *Flames and Smoke Visible* non-stop, in a space of a few hours—I was totally caught up in the drama of fire fighting. With the authority of experience as a fire fighter, and the talent and the skill honed as the author of many brilliant novels, Mr. Lliteras has produced a beautifully written, riveting account about this profession that is not only a first-rate entertaining book but also a book which informs, instructs, and allows the reader access to the human heart."

—David Willson, author of *REMF Diary: A Novel of the Vietnam War Zone* and editor of *Viet Nam War Generation Journal*

D0180387

Also by D.S. Lliteras

FLAMES
AND
SMOKE
VISIBLE

A Fire Fighter's Tale

D.S. LLITERAS

RAINBOW RIDGE
BOOKS

Cover and interior design by Frame 25 Productions
Cover photograph © Dmitry Pistrov c/o Shutterstock.com

Published by:
Rainbow Ridge Books, LLC
140 Rainbow Ridge Road
Faber, Virginia 22938
434-361-1723

If you are unable to order this book from your local
bookseller, you may order directly from the distributor.

Square One Publishers, Inc.
115 Herricks Road
Garden City Park, NY 11040
Phone: (516) 535-2010
Fax: (516) 535-2014
Toll-free: 877-900-BOOK

Visit the author at:

Library of Congress Cataloging-in-Publication Data applied for.

ISBN 978-1-937907-09-9

10 9 8 7 6 5 4 3 2 1

Printed on acid-free recycled paper in the United States of America

Dedicated to America Díaz Lliteras

CONTENTS

INTRODUCTION

I AM A FIRE FIGHTER—that is, I was a fire fighter for the city of Norfolk, Virginia. I am presently retired and I am an active member of the International Association of Fire Fighters (IAFF), Local 68 (AFL-CIO). And the day that changed my life was the night the brass hit and woke me up around 3 a.m. at Fire Station 15. The dispatcher announced a 10-1 house fire at an address located in the Ocean View district of Norfolk.

As soon as I swung my legs over the side of my bed and stood up, I knew there was something wrong with me. I was not right. I was not myself. In fact, I collapsed during that incident and was transported from the fireground to a hospital in an ambulance.

Suddenly, that night, I was on the other side of my occupation.

That night, I surrendered to a darkness of some unknown length of time. Enough time, however, to have the four top ranking chiefs of the Fire Department appear at my bedside in a hospital's emergency room.

"Damn," I said when I woke up. "Am I dead?"

I heard laughter and reassurance. I saw smiles and concern. Then I realized that I was going to be alright.

That incident was the catalyst that later inspired me to write, *Flames and Smoke Visible*—to write about what it means "to be."

Every person at some time or another asks what it means to be. What does it mean to be a son, what does it mean to be a mother, what does it mean to be an adult, a nurse, a soldier.

Fire fighters by necessity must enter homes in order to save lives or property. They see people at their most vulnerable—what does it mean to be when a person's privacy or dignity has been compromised?

A fire fighter sees more death and destruction than the average person. Asking the question—what it means to be—is almost inescapable. What does it means to be when a person has survived a fire but has lost all of his possessions? Our possessions are an extension of who we are; they define a person—at least in part. In the aftermath of a fire, all that may remain is the skeleton of dreams— the charred remnant of a work of art or a child's toy. What is it to be without an irreplaceable Bible that chronicled generations of a family's births and marriages and deaths. What is it to be without the treasures that trace a person's past.

Fire fighters are often present at that moment between life and death—what does it mean to be when you are dying; what does it mean to be when you are no longer, because even in not being there is still being in having been.

And sometimes it is the fire fighter himself who survives, thanks to the labors of the men and women he works with. I am such a survivor. And I had to ask myself the question, what does it mean to be when you can no longer do the job you love?

In answering that question, I had to look backward at who I had been. These are some of the stories as I remember them.

I also had to deal with the present and part of that present was spent in the hospital sharing a room with another man—a man who had no memory. He could only live in the present—and even that was a confabulation. He was nineteen one moment; he had a son nineteen the next. Yesterday he had been in Egypt; tomorrow he was going to be a race car driver. He could describe events in vivid detail. Although he was a tragic case, he at times exhibited an infectious sense of joy. What was it to be a person with no memory, no past, no future, and only a fictitious present?

A fire fighter has many opportunities to ask that question—what does it mean to be? Perhaps they ask the question more than other people, but they have no more answers than anyone else.

Everything in this book is factually true. The time sequences, however, have been compressed and altered for structural and dramatic purposes and the names and places have been changed to protect the identities of those involved in the incidences that I have written about—fire fighters and paramedics, police officers and arson investigators, citizens and victims. In the final analysis, this book is a remembrance of things past with the flaws that all remembrances are vulnerable to.

I loved that life on the fireground. And I loved having worked with all those professionals who safeguard our streets. They are my people—fine people, who place their lives on the line every time they are on duty to protect the citizens of this nation. It is a war that is waged every day and in every city in this country—a war that is generally ignored by most citizens until they are directly involved in it. Until then, those of us who are employed in public safety are taken for granted. And, I suppose, that is a worthy testament concerning how well we do our jobs, which is also as good a place as any to end this introduction.

D. S. Lliteras
October, 2012

1

FIRST-IN ENGINE

THE CLANG OF THE brass assaulted me, and the intrusion of the dispatcher's voice, announcing a house-fire, pulled me from the depths of my slumber.

I recognized the address. I knew we were going to be the first-in engine. Then why was I still in my rack? I wondered.

I finally sat up on my bed, feeling strange and heavy and oddly distant from my surroundings. I had to get moving, I thought.

The other two fire fighters in the bunkroom were already half dressed and shuffling across the room.

"Come on, Danny," said Ric, as Sam pushed open the double doors leading to the apparatus floor. "We've got a run!"

I threw my blanket aside and stood up, as Ric followed Sam through the doors. Then I grabbed my trousers from the nearby chair. As I struggled to get them on, I had a weird feeling that I had left a part of myself in bed. I felt half spirited. Incomplete. Strained.

I listened for the sound of the diesel engine. As long as the engine wasn't running, I had time, even though firehouse time at two in the morning was always distorted. I heard the forward apparatus door opening.

I buckled my belt, picked up my shoes and sweatshirt, and stumbled toward the double doors like an incomplete ghost. The engine started as soon as I stepped onto the apparatus floor.

I heard the right side-door slam shut as I trotted to the left side of the engine. I threw my shoes and sweatshirt into the jump seat compartment, then climbed onboard with tremendous effort.

The engine crept out of the station and onto the apron and waited for the captain to climb into the right side of the cab, after he pressed the switch to lower the forward apparatus door.

I was already in my turnout pants and boots, and I was struggling to raise my red suspenders over my shoulders, when the engine made an explosive left turn from the station's apron onto Fishermans Road. I leaned into the turn, as I reached for my turnout coat. Then the engine made an immediate hard right onto Sturgis Road and threw me off balance. I grabbed the back of the jump seat in front of me with one hand, to prevent myself from falling, as I continued struggling into my coat with the other.

I felt as if I were encased in syrup, but I kept moving.

"I think we got one," Ric said.

I nodded. I lacked my usual enthusiasm.

"Engine Fifteen, dispatcher."

The captain keyed his radio. "Engine Fifteen, go ahead."

"Report of flames and smoke visible."

"Ten-four."

"See? I knew it," said Ric.

With my turnout coat finally buttoned, I reached down into the jump seat, found my SCBA cylinder valve, and cranked it open. The tank bell sang out and the high pressure hose stiffened. Then I sat down in the jump seat and inserted my arms through the straps of the tank's harness.

The movement of the engine through the night-lit streets, the constant wail of the siren, the intermittent blast of the air-horn, and the frequent transmissions from the dispatcher engulfed me.

I draped the facemask's harness around my neck, pulled my shoulder straps tight, then fastened and adjusted my waist strap. I brought the facepiece to my ear and cracked open my mainline regulator valve. After I was comforted by the air flow, I shut the valve. I put on my helmet, hooked a smoke cutter onto my left shoulder strap, placed my portable radio in my turnout coat pocket, adjusted my Nomex hood around my neck, buttoned my collar, gloved up, and inhaled gratefully for getting ready in time, despite my distorted composure.

"It's on my side, Danny," said Ric, as soon as we turned onto the street that led to our final destination. Smoke was in the air.

"I smell it," I said.

"Get the irons."

"Right."

As soon as the engine stopped, Ric threw open his side-door, unhooked the nozzle from its cradle, and ran toward a narrow alley between an apartment complex and a house. I unlatched, from the rear interior bulkhead, a halligan tool that was married to a flathead axe by a short length of Velcro wrapped midway around their handles, and carefully stepped off the piece. The irons felt extremely heavy. Odd, I thought.

I grabbed the hoseline just as the third section began to clear the bed and headed in Ric's direction. As soon as I felt the rest of the hoseline clear the bed, I realized the line was too short—so did Sam. I dropped the taut line and hurried to Ric's side.

Flames leaped outside through the rear windows and back door from the burning interior.

"Where's the water!?" Ric hollered.

I pulled off my gloves. "It's coming!" I was certain that Sam, our driver, was breaking the line to add another section of hose. "Tank up!"

I threw back my helmet, letting it hang from my neck by the chin-strap, then donned my facepiece, turned on my air at the regulator, pulled my Nomex hood over my head, screwed my helmet back on, tightened my chin-strap, raised and Velcroed my turnout coat collar, slipped on my gloves, and positioned myself behind Ric, near the door, to go inside.

The interior looked hot. Vicious fingers of narrow flame extended from the main fire through the broken windows and the open door.

"Where's the damn water!?" Ric shouted through his facemask, which muted his voice.

"Sam had to break the line!"

"Oh! Right!" Ric calmed down.

We waited patiently.

As soon as the hose tightened, Ric cracked open the nozzle to bleed the charged line and adjust the nozzle's pattern. When I tapped him on the back to let him know I was ready, he fully opened the nozzle and directed the water stream into the open doorway.

We fought our way through the entrance into a short hallway and turned left into the nearest room, where we knocked down the fire. Then we turned around and went back through the hall-way into another room, where we knocked down more fire. When the fire rekindled behind us, we turned around and aggressively attacked it. As the backup man, I hauled on the line to give Ric slack, and as the nozzle man, he directed the water onto the fire.

Suddenly, the steamed interior became black and quiet. Ric shut down the line and waited for more fire.

When the hot, smoky darkness persisted, we knew this had been a hard and fast stop. So fast, that the second-in engine company hadn't reached us yet.

"Good stop, Ric!"

"Yeah!"

"Yee-haa!"

"Go, boy!"

As we continued to wait for another rekindle, I felt my chest begin to tighten. When I tried to inhale, I realized I couldn't breathe.

At first, I thought someone was playing a practical joke, that the second-in engine company was on the scene and that one of those boys was surreptitiously pinching my low pressure air hose. But I knew better. I would have heard them if they were inside.

The increased pressure in my chest accompanied my continued inability to breathe. I gasped. I dropped the hoseline. I reached for my chest with my left hand; the pressure felt as if an elephant was standing on it.

I told Ric I had to go outside. I couldn't wait for him to decipher my garbled voice, caused by the facemask. The fire was out and he was safe and—I had to go outside.

I followed the line to the door and stepped outside where I threw back my helmet, pulled my Nomex hood down around my neck, tore off my facepiece, and unbuckled my waist strap to drop my tank. Then I unhooked my helmet's chin-strap and my facemask's neck strap from around my neck and dropped both items to the ground.

I leaned against a nearby parked car feeling confident that this strange episode was going to go away. But the pressure in my chest increased and my breathing became more difficult. Then, as if someone turned off a switch inside of me, I found myself on my hands and knees, feeling weak and disconnected. When I blinked my eyes and saw the individual grains of dirt on the ground, it finally occurred to me that I was having a heart attack.

I raised my weary head, saw my captain, and muttered, "Chest pains," before I completely collapsed to the ground.

I felt the hands of a dozen fire fighters carrying me to an ambulance. I heard a multitude of familiar voices uttering my name. I saw another form of darkness, as I received a barrage of reassurances.

2

RESCUE THIRTEEN

From my supine perspective, the ambulance's interior seemed smaller. And in response to this strange confinement, I strained against the straps that secured me to the stretcher. I tried to sit up.

"Take it easy, Danny."

A firm hand pressed my left shoulder down, forcing me to relax. I glanced to my left and saw Mark Harris sitting next to me; he was on the telephone, speaking to the doctor-on-duty. He hung up the phone and reached over me to fetch something from a small compartment. Chris Macklin, the other paramedic, was preparing to start an IV on me. The bag was already hanging from an overhead hook with a clear, plastic spaghetti line attached to it. Chris unwrapped a needle from a sterile package and handed it to Mark, which prompted Mark to lay the flat, white package that he obtained from the small compartment on my chest.

"Is this Rescue Thirteen?" I asked.

"Sure is. Concentrate on your breathing, Danny."

I adjusted the oxygen non-rebreathing mask on my face with my right hand while Mark stuck the top of my left hand with the needle. I closed my eyes.

Mark had the needle taped into place and had the IV running by the time I opened my eyes.

"Relax, Danny," said Chris. "You're going to be alright, brother." He removed my hand from the non-rebreather, which was held to my face with an elastic band, and guided my hand down to my side. Then I felt Mark pressing something that felt like tape against my bare upper chest.

"What's that?"

"A nitro patch," said Mark. He turned to Chris. "Let's get rolling."

Chris stepped outside, through the rear of the ambulance, and closed the door.

I took a deep breath.

"How do you feel?"

I looked at Mark. "I don't know. Surprised. Weird."

"How weird?"

"My arms and legs." I felt the jolt of the ambulance's movement. "They're tingling." It felt strange riding in this tiny box that squeaked and rattled.

"Tingling, you say?"

"Yeah. They feel—I—they, they feel numb and tingly." I felt every bump and turn in the street, every—

"Your arms and legs."

I nodded. "God."

"What?"

"I can't believe this is happening."

"On a scale of one to ten, with ten the most severe, how do you rate your chest pains?"

"I don't know. I—"

"Try."

I closed my eyes to measure my pain. "Seven, I guess."

"Seven."

"Or eight. Something like that. It's the pressure."

"You still have the pressure?"

"Not as badly. The O_2 helped."

"Do you have a headache?"

"Headache?" I reached out for one. "No. No headache. God. I still can't believe this is happening to me, Mark."

"Don't worry. You're going to be alright. Try to relax."

I smiled weakly. "Aren't you at Station Seven?"

"Yeah. I'm filling in at Thirteen tonight. They stuck me on the box."

"I'm sorry."

"That's alright. I'm glad I'm here for you."

"Thanks."

The ambulance hit a pothole. The vehicle shook and rattled violently.

"It's weird," I said.

"You feel weird? Where?"

"No." I looked at Mark, as I gathered the strength to speak. "It feels weird to be on the other end of this." Then I closed my eyes, suddenly overcome with exhaustion. I felt a stethoscope against my chest. I felt the increased tightness of a blood pressure cuff around my right upper arm. I felt—I felt things—things, were going on all around me, with or without my understanding.

I drifted. I wished I was back with my engine company. They still had a long night ahead of them. First ventilation and investigation, then salvage and overhaul, followed by gathering equipment and repacking hose. It would be quite some time before Engine Fifteen would be cleared. The first-in engine was almost always the last engine cleared from a scene.

I loved the fireground. I hated admitting that to anyone. I loved the skills involved and the hard, physical work and the professional comradery.

I drifted. I imagined that the incident was over and we were riding through the dark and deserted neighborhood streets of Ocean View, heading back to our station.

I drifted. I was back on the job. All those years of fire fighting raced through my mind as I lay there not knowing what lay in my future—if I had one.

3

HOSE PACKING

Seven sections of hoseline were stacked inside the jump seat compartment: four sections on my side and three sections on Ric's side. Dawn was approaching.

"There's no more sleep for us tonight," said Ric.

"You've got that right," I said.

Sam drove the engine several feet past the station, then stopped to shift into reverse as the captain pressed the apparatus door opener that was clipped onto the engine cab's sun visor. Because the streets were vacant, Ric and I did not bother to get off the piece to direct traffic.

As soon as Sam backed the engine into the station and engaged the parking brakes, Ric and I opened the side-door to our jump seat compartment and stepped off the engine.

The captain keyed the radio. "Engine Fifteen's in quarters."

"Ten-four, Engine Fifteen."

I went to the rear of the station and pressed the switch to the overhead door. As soon as the door rose a few feet, I saw Bear standing at the threshold. "Hey there, big boy." I crouched toward him. "What are you doing here so early in the morning?"

Bear did not respond to human presence like most dogs. He did not jump or pant or wag his tail.

"What do we have here at this hour?" said Ric, as he approached the rear of the station to throw a smile at Bear.

"Reckon he's hungry?" I said.

"Reckon so."

"I'll give him some of that leftover chicken."

"Don't give him any bone."

"I know better."

I went into the galley while Ric went back to the engine to unload the wet and dirty, rolled hose.

"I'll be right out to help you, Ric."

"Throw some coffee on while you're in there, too."

"Right."

Bear followed me to the galley's door, but he remained on the apparatus floor. He never entered any of our living quarters no matter how much we coaxed him to.

Bear was a wary dog. A neglected creature. Mean to the bone, if provoked. He was short and stout, dirty and mangy, black and hairy, wide-faced and inscrutable: he looked like a black bear, hence, his firehouse name.

I opened the refrigerator, took two chicken breasts off a plate, and pulled the meat off the bone. After I wiped my hands off on a paper towel, I looked through the Plexiglas of the galley's aluminum framed door and saw Bear sitting patiently on the apparatus floor.

"I'm coming," I said.

I filled a porcelain bowl with water, pushed open the door with my foot, and set the bowl of water and handful of meat on the floor in front of Bear.

He sniffed the chicken, then carefully probed the meat with his black tongue.

"Are you doing alright, old boy?"

Bear looked at me as if he were waiting for me to go back into the galley so he could eat his meal undisturbed.

"You poor creature. One of these days I'm going to know something about you." I pulled open the galley's door and held it open, momentarily. "Where do you go when you leave here? What do you do? Poor thing. Go on, eat."

Ric walked past us with a fifty-foot section of dirty hose dangling from each hand.

"I'll be right with you, Ric."

"Make some coffee, first."

"Right." I went back into the galley and started a pot of coffee. When I heard the dispatcher's voice come over the air through the galley's speakers, I realized the monitor wasn't reset. I went into the watchroom beside the galley, reset the monitor, glanced through the Plexiglas of the watchroom's door leading to the apparatus floor, and saw Sam helping Ric unload the dirty hose. So, I went into the hose room and lifted two straight, rolled sections of clean inch-and-three-quarters hose off the rack. I carried them to the rear of the station, lay the rolls flat on the apparatus floor, grabbed the female couplings, and pulled them to unwind the hose and pay-out the line to the side of the engine in preparation for packing.

We were exhausted and sweat-soaked; our tee shirts clung to us like wet rags. Ric and the captain had soot coating the sides of their faces and the insides of their ears. I knew these fireground countenances were an accurate reflection of myself.

As I walked back to the hose room, the inside of my nose began to itch. I stopped, pulled out the paper towel that I'd stuffed into my trouser pocket while I was in the galley making coffee, and blew my nose. When I spread open the paper towel with both hands, I saw a black, wet glob of mucus soaked into the paper towel. I studied the contents as if I were analyzing the abstract image of a Rorschach inkblot test.

"Hmm."

Ric brushed past me on his way to the hose room. "What the hell are you doing there, boy?"

"I'm looking at my lost future."

"Your what?"

"This reflects another day that I've lost from my life." I showed him my black-and-white Rorschach image.

"Damn." He twitched his nose, wiped his own blackened nostrils with the back of his hand, and looked at the sticky smear on his skin. "This ain't nothin'."

"That's one day closer to your reward," I said.

"Yeah, well—go on, now." He wiped the back of his hand on his trousers. "I ain't listenin' to another one of your crazy head-trips."

Sam came out of the hose room and dropped a pair of clean, rolled hose on the floor. "We all got to go sometime."

"I ain't listenin' to either one of you."

Sam chuckled. Then he grabbed both female couplings and started paying-out the lines toward the left side of the engine.

I continued to grin at Ric as I wadded the paper towel and shoved it back into my pocket.

Ric shook his head as he grinned. "You're crazy." Then he went into the hose room.

After I realized there was enough line payed-out on the apparatus floor to start packing, I turned around, approached the engine, climbed up its side, stepped into the basket, and opened the lid to the cross-lay hosebed.

The captain came out of his office. "You need any help?"

"Damn. Are you done with your paper work, already?" I said.

The captain climbed onto the left side of the piece and Ric climbed onto the right side. Since the engine was built so high, it was impossible to pack hose while standing alongside the piece. So, they had to put on safety harnesses and hook into the side to free their hands to work the line.

I lay down on the roof of the engine's cab in a prone position, with my head and arms hovering over the hosebed, so I would be free to work the line across the bed. Sam remained on the apparatus floor to provide slack on the line as we packed the engine.

Despite our dull-headedness, we carefully flaked the clean hose back and forth across the beds.

"Iron man," muttered by either Sam or the captain, indicated the need to couple the next hose section, signaled the approach of the joined couplings, and provided the only pause to the repetitious act of hose packing.

"It's going to be a long day," said Ric.

"Are you working your part-time job today?" I asked.

"Every day. I'm painting a house."

"I'm driving an oil truck, these days," Sam chimed from below.

"I've got an officer's meeting to go to downtown," said Ron, our captain. "What about you, Danny?"

"I've got a deadline to meet."

"You've written a new book?"

"Yeah. It's in the copyediting stage."

"Lord," said Sam, "give me an oil truck to drive any day."

"You've got that right," Ric added. "Paper work ain't for me. All I'd do is fall asleep."

"Nah. You'd get used to it, like anything else."

"You reckon?" Ric tilted his head thoughtfully. "I don't know."

"Sure," I said.

"Brother, that coffee is going to taste mighty good."

"Amen to that."

We finished packing the engine, then made sure all the tools and SCBA tanks and personal equipment were back in place and ready to go for the next alarm, before the captain keyed the radio and went on the air to put us back in commission.

"Fresh pot," Sam hollered over the intercom, even though it was unnecessary to remind anybody that there was coffee made.

We shuffled into the galley like mindless ghosts and bunched around the coffee pot, holding large ceramic cups as empty as ourselves. Ron reached the pot first and was kind enough to pour. Then each of us tended to our own steaming cup: Ric liked Cremora and sugar, Sam and I liked milk if there was any left in the refrigerator, and the captain liked his black.

Then we congregated around the galley table and drank our coffee and talked about the fire incident: what went right and what went wrong. We joked and we laughed and we felt pride in our work without admitting it.

But none of that happened, I thought, when the jolt of the ambulance startled me out of my dream-filled torpor state. I was still strapped in a stretcher and trapped inside an ambulance that was transporting me toward an unknown future.

4

EMERGENCY ROOM

The sound of the backing-bell indicated to me that Chris was positioning the ambulance near the emergency room's entrance. Shortly after the vehicle came to a stop and the backing-bell quit, Chris raised the ambulance's rear door, raised the bumper-step, and positioned himself at the foot of the stretcher to assist Mark.

Chris winked at me. "Hey there, partner."

Mark transferred the O_2 line supplying my nonrebreather to a portable cylinder attached to the side of the stretcher. "Relax." He disconnected me from the blood pressure cuff and unhooked the IV bag from the overhead. "Keep your arms inside the stretcher."

As soon as Mark positioned himself near the head of the stretcher, Chris pushed in the side-release and pulled the stretcher through the opening until the bottom of the stretcher engaged the safety catch and jerked the contraption to an abrupt stop. Then the stretcher shuddered when Chris released its wheel carriage.

Mark stepped out of the ambulance as Chris unhooked the stretcher from the safety catch. Together, they artfully navigated the clumsy contraption toward the large, glass double door of the emergency room.

At the entrance, Chris had to punch a number code into a cipher-lock, then press a button. When the doors swung open, they rolled me into a phosphorescent-lit world of sterile stainless steel that appeared shadowless and felt cold.

I was wheeled into a space, defined by curtains, and transferred from the stretcher to a bed by Chris and Mark and two nurses. Then I was hooked to a monitor and a blood pressure cuff, questioned and probed by a doctor, then a nurse, then another doctor, then another nurse, who gave me four baby aspirin, which I chewed and swallowed down as she transferred my O_2 line from the portable cylinder to the hospital's floor unit.

I was stuck in the arm with a needle in order to get several tubes of blood out of me, then they took my temperature and x-rayed me. I never got a chance to thank Chris and Mark before they left.

I floated within the whirlwind of this alien world, wishing I was at home or back at the station.

I drifted.

5

FILL-INS

THE REAR OVERHEAD DOOR exposing the apparatus floor was open when I drove onto Station Fifteen's parking lot. Judging by the vehicles that were parked in the lot, the crazy B-shift had been relieved and all but Johnson, their cook, had either gone home or gone to their part-time jobs.

Johnson was smoking a cigar and drinking a cup of coffee and fuming about something. I knew his agitated state probably had something to do with a new fire department policy. He was an old-timer who hated change, but he was a damn good fire fighter. Everything got under Johnson's skin; he was a real hothead, but his heart was in the right place.

I parked my car, grabbed my personal station-bag, and greeted Johnson as I got out of my car.

"Good morning, Johnson. What's your no good?"

"You don't want to know." He puffed hard on his cigar, then grunted.

"That bad?"

He yanked the cigar out of his mouth and spilled some of his coffee. "Don't get me started. You'll hear about it soon enough in the galley."

"You've got three beautiful days off ahead of you," I said optimistically.

"Don't I know it," he said. "Don't I know it." His eyes darkened. He drank some of his coffee, then puffed hard on his cigar. "I'm out of here." He tossed the remains of his coffee into the grass as he headed for his pickup truck.

"Take care," I said, feeling lucky that I didn't have to listen to the details of his inner turmoil.

I went to my boot locker, took out my turnout gear, and deposited everything on the apparatus floor, including my station-bag, near the left side of the engine. Then I went into the galley to get a cup of coffee and find out what the day was going to be like.

T. C. and the captain were sitting at the table, Sam was leaning against the sink drinking his coffee, and Ric was making a fresh pot.

"Who's got the fill-in?" I asked.

"I do," T. C. answered.

"And what's the B-shift griping about now?"

"Uniforms."

"Damn. Not that again," I said. "Hurry up with that coffee, Ric."

"I'm doin' the best I can."

I got two clean cups out of the drawer and handed one to him.

"We've got school inspections today," said Ron, our captain.

I grimaced. School inspections were terribly dull.

"Let's knock them out this morning, if we can," Sam suggested.

"Good idea," I said. "What do you think, Cap?"

"Works for me. I hate missing my afternoon nap."

I sat down at the table, set my cup down, and waited for coffee. "Where are they sending you, T. C.?"

"I'm filling in at Nine."

"Twenty-four?"

T. C. nodded as he displayed a little frown. Most fire fighters disliked fill-ins, including myself.

Fill-ins were a way of adjusting manpower to stations that had personnel on leave. At a fire station, all the positions had to be filled and it was each battalion chief's job, in the three districts, to temporarily transfer excess fire fighters from one station to another within their district, or to transfer them between districts, or to pay time-and-a-half to acquire additional personnel, called hirebacks, from the other two off-duty shifts when necessary. That was the administrative side of things. On the human side, it worked like this:

When a fire fighter reports to his station for duty and finds out that he's up for the fill-in, he has to go to his bedroom-locker and pack his bedroll and shove his shaving kit into his personal station-bag and throw these items in his car along with his turnout gear. Then he has to drive to whatever station he's been assigned to for either twelve or twenty-four hours, depending on the length of the leave vacancy; he may have to spend a twelve-hour day-trick at one station and a twelve-hour night-trick at another. A twelve-hour day is called a half-trick and a twenty-four-hour day is called a full-trick. Hopefully, his fill-in station is within the district, since he knows those fire fighters better. But sometimes, he has to go to a station outside of his district where he has to reacquaint himself with some of the guys.

Depending on the number of pieces there are at the station he's sent to and depending on his professional qualifications, he can be assigned to an engine or a ladder or a squad or a rescue unit; and he can be given the position of fire fighter, acting operator, or acting officer on any of the pieces. After he secures his assigned position and throws his turnout gear onboard, if he's smart and he's there for a full-trick, he'll find out what beds are available in the bunkroom and lay claim to one of them with his bedroll and overnight station-bag.

Since he's missed morning lineup, the fill-in man has to find out what his morning housecleaning duties are through the lieutenant, if it's a large multiple piece station, or through the house captain, if it's a single piece station. Then he finds the cook and pays him six dollars for that day's lunch and dinner; it's best not to ask the cook what he plans to serve.

The culture shock is usually over once his turnout gear is in its designated jump seat, his bedroll is on an unassigned bed, the cook's been paid, his morning cleanup is completed, and the officer of the day has acknowledged his existence. From here on, it's pure human relations with less familiar fire fighters, but the work is the same: respond to fire and paramedic calls and perform whatever collateral duties that may or may not be assigned for the day like hydrant inspections, school inspections, pre-fire planning inspections, hose testing, washing the pieces, and a wide variety of hands-on and classroom training.

I smiled at T. C. "At least you're in our district."

He nodded. "You're right. It could be worse."

"Just tell the boys at Nine not to worry about any fires," Ric said. "Tell them Engine Fifteen will take care of them."

"That'll get them wound up," Sam added.

But I knew T. C. wouldn't. T. C. was our rookie fire fighter with less than a year in the department. He was soft-spoken and still wary of the veteran fire fighters, like most timid rookies. I liked T. C. and I made it a point to encourage his friendship and trust; I never forgot my own uncertain days as a rookie.

Ric leaned over my right side and poured me some coffee. "There you go, big boy."

"Thanks." I got up from the table to check the refrigerator for milk when the brass hit.

"Car fire. Engine Fifteen respond to 8300 Chesapeake Boulevard on a car fire. Time out: 0640."

"That's on the corner of Sheppard Avenue and Chesapeake," Sam casually remarked, as he got up with the rest of us.

We headed for the engine, leaving T. C. to his fill-in. He knew to lock up the station for us before he left.

6

CAR FIRE

SAM STARTED THE ENGINE and turned on the emergency running lights, while Ric and I got into our turnout gear. As soon as the captain stepped into his nightpants and boots, he climbed into the cab and keyed the radio. "Engine Fifteen's responding."

"Ten-four, Engine Fifteen."

Sam drove the engine onto the paved apron in front of the station, checked the flow of traffic, then made a left onto Fishermans Road. The captain turned on the siren as Sam accelerated the engine.

By the time we reached Chesapeake Boulevard, I had my turnout coat buttoned and my Nomex hood and helmet on. Sheppard Avenue was a half-dozen streets away. As soon as Sam made a hard right, I stood up and peered over the back of the jump seat. I saw black smoke.

"It's on my side," I said to Ric, as I slipped on my gloves.

"Right." Ric stood up to see for himself. "Damn, she's lit off good."

"Yeah." I tightened my helmet chin-strap.

Ric and I and the captain were buttoned down and ready, but none of us tanked-up. Most veteran fire fighters still did not don their SCBA tanks at car fires because this added equipment decreased a fire fighter's mobility around the burning vehicle. The rationale was: as long as you stayed upwind, there was plenty of good air; and as long as you held your breath, when you had to step into the smoke, you were alright.

The burning vehicle had been driven off the road and abandoned.

"Driver's door is open," said Ric. "I reckon everybody's out."

"I hope so," I said. "Look! There's a lady standing on the grass. She's waving at us."

"She looks alright to me. Good."

A police car sped toward the scene from the opposite direction.

Since the burning vehicle stood fifty feet from the intersection, facing south, Sam took a left on Sheppard Avenue to cross Chesapeake Boulevard's wide, grassy median, then turned right into the traffic where he pulled off the road and spotted the engine facing the fully involved vehicle.

The captain keyed the radio. "Engine Fifteen's on the scene."

"Ten-four, Engine Fifteen."

Thick black smoke billowed from the car. Flames shot out from under the front and two sides of the vehicle, and fire engulfed the passenger's interior.

I opened my side-door, unhooked the nozzle, pulled it out of the cradle, and stepped off the piece as Sam placed the engine into pump gear. Ric followed me out through the same door to avoid the dangerous traffic on his side.

As I laid the first section of line toward the vehicle, Ric went to the left-side engine compartment to get a halligan tool and a pry bar. Sam jumped out of the cab and went to the pump panel to drop the tank, and the captain climbed out of the cab and approached the lady, who was standing too close to her burning vehicle.

As soon as Ric helped me pay-out the second section of line, Sam broke the line and hooked it to the side of the engine. The captain stood by and assessed the scene for safety, directed the lady to step further away from her burning vehicle, and encouraged the police officer to direct traffic. The captain also kept an eye on our method of attack in case he needed to issue a command. But additional orders were generally unnecessary because of our individual years of experience, as well as our fireground experiences as a company. Each man knew what hole to fill, which meant knowing what task to step into that would help the other fire fighter get the job done.

I pulled down my helmet's faceshield and waited for Sam to charge the line, as I stood by the right side of the vehicle, away from the road. As soon as the hose tightened, I cracked the nozzle open, bled the line, adjusted the nozzle setting to a medium angle fog pattern, then aimed the shut-off nozzle toward the vehicle.

Ric lay the irons on the ground and grabbed hold of the line, several feet behind me, as my backup.

I pulled open the nozzle and directed the water stream at the car and started sweeping out the fire from underneath the vehicle. As soon as I knocked down the flames that were impinging on the gas tank, I briefly hit the interior, then I worked the line toward the front and diverted the fire stream over the hood, to cool down the grill and engine compartment, so the hood could be opened up.

Ric dropped the line and approached the opened driver's door, as I continued to direct the water stream at whatever fire remained. He reached inside the door to find the hood release but discovered that the cable was burned through when he pulled the release.

By this time, Sam had thrown on his turnout coat and helmet and was standing beside me with the halligan tool that Ric had staged nearby. I shut down the nozzle and stepped aside to let Sam force open the hood. Heavy smoke was still spewing from the vehicle.

Ric joined Sam with the pry bar and I stood by with the line. Sam wedged the fork of the halligan tool near the hood latch and pushed down. Then Ric stabbed the partial opening, provided by the halligan tool, with the point of his pry bar and pushed up. By applying brute force in opposite directions, they managed to expose the hood latch. Sam disengaged the halligan tool and Ric stabbed the chiseled end of the pry bar against the exposed hood latch until the hood popped open.

I carefully directed the water stream into the engine compartment as Ric cautiously lifted the hood. Sam quickly propped the heel of his halligan tool on top of the radiator, allowing Ric to lower the hood until it rested on the fork of the upright tool to keep the hood open. Then Ric and Sam stepped out of my way as I fully opened the nozzle to drown what was left of the fire.

I shut down the nozzle to conserve water and stepped back. "What do you think?"

"Looks like we got her," Ric said.

"Yeah." I peered at the captain. "What do you think?"

"Good job."

"There's still plenty of water left in the tank," Sam said.

"Then let's drown it," said the captain.

"Right." I pulled the nozzle halfway open and directed the water stream back over the burned-out engine.

Ric pulled the keys out of the ignition, went to the rear of the vehicle, and opened the trunk, while Sam unlocked the other doors and opened them. The captain peered under the hood to determine the cause of the fire, before he approached the vehicle's owner and the police officer to gather additional information for his fire report.

By the time I finished flooding the destRiced automobile from hood to trunk, the captain managed to record the vehicle's license and registration numbers, attain the lady's address and phone number, and receive an ETA from the dispatcher concerning a tow truck.

The automobile was a four-door Dodge Omni. Much of its cranberry color was blackened and its interior was gutted. Under the hood, all the plastic parts and wiring were melted and fused over the four-cylinder, aluminum engine block.

I shut down the line and laid the nozzle on the ground as soon as I heard the change in the engine's idle, indicating that the water tank was empty. "I hope she has insurance."

"She won't get much for this old thing," Sam said, as he reduced the pump's pressure at the panel and pushed in the tank lever.

Ric shook his head sympathetically. "Nobody ever gets ahead. Nobody."

7

FIRE CHIEFS

SOMEONE PULLED OFF MY oxygen nonrebreather and replaced it with a cannula. When I opened my eyes, I saw five chiefs from the fire department and a captain gathered at the foot of my bed.

"Whoa," I said. "Where's the angel?" The nurse standing at the side of my bed stuck a thermometer into my mouth. "Am I dead?" I mumbled.

The nurse smiled. The chiefs chuckled.

I squirmed in my bed. "I'm not important—" The nurse pulled the thermometer out of my mouth and studied the reading. "I'm not important enough to have all this brass standing at my bedside." She recorded my temperature in a chart.

"You're important to us," the director of the fire department said, as he placed his right hand on my ankle to reassure me.

A couple of the chiefs shuffled aside to allow the nurse to get past them and proceed to her next patient. Battalion Chief Tasha Jenkins leaned over my right side with sympathetic eyes. "You're going to be alright."

"God, I can't believe this is happening to me."

"It can happen to anybody," Chief McCann said.

"That's right," said Chief Swisher, my shift commander. "And don't worry, the department's going to take care of you."

"You can be sure of that," said Director Haufman.

Chief Neville and my old friend, Captain Leon Walker, who was the department's safety officer, enthusiastically agreed.

"Is there anything we can do?" Leon asked.

"You can get me out of here," I said.

They laughed.

"You relax," Chief Swisher ordered. "There's no use in you tryin' to bust out of here before they have a handle on your condition."

"God, I can't believe this. It was a good, hard stop," I said. "We had the fire knocked down in no time."

"What happened?" Director Haufman asked.

I told them what had happened in the greatest detail I was capable of at the time. They seemed interested and genuinely concerned.

"Is there anything we can do?" Chief Jenkins asked. "Do you want me to call Kathleen?"

"God, no, Chief. Don't tell her at this hour of the night. There's nothing she can do, right now, but worry." I noticed Chief Swisher and Chief McCann nodding with understanding. "You know how it is. There's no use dragging my wife out of bed." I turned my attention back to Chief Jenkins. "Thanks, Chief. I'll call her in the morning."

"Just let me know what you want, and you've got it."

I smiled. Tasha was my battalion chief and a close friend and a damn good egg who always took care of her boys. I was glad she was here.

The portable radios hanging from the belts of everybody around me toned-out and demanded everyone's attention. The dispatcher announced a fire alarm that deployed a full complement, then confirmed another working fire that required an additional engine and ladder company.

Chief Swisher tugged at my feet. "You're going to be alright."

"We've got to go," said Chief McCann.

"Take care." I knew Director Haufman wanted to leave, so I nodded to him. "Thanks, Chief."

Haufman took the cue. "Yes. Two working fires and an alarm. You stay here until the doctors have cleared you."

"I will." I looked at Chief McCann and Chief Swisher. "Thanks."

A doctor, dressed in a three-piece suit, maneuvered around the three departing chiefs. They shambled away from my bedside and disappeared behind the curtains that defined my emergency room space.

"I'm Dr. Rifkin."

"Hello, Doc. What have we got?"

Without hesitation or expression, he delivered the news that my signs and symptoms made it necessary that they perform a heart catheterization to find out what was wrong with me. He supported his casual presentation with some convoluted medical jargon.

"Okay, Doc, I'm ready. Let's get started."

Then came the bad news.

He told me I had to stay in the hospital for the weekend because the catheterization couldn't be scheduled until Monday morning.

"No, no, no," I said, as I squirmed in my bed. "There's no way I'm spending the weekend in this place. No way. No way. Can't I go home and come back Monday?"

The doctor shook his head. "We've got to keep you in here for observation."

I shifted my attention to Chief Jenkins, hoping to appeal to her softhearted nature, but she wouldn't let me.

"Do what the doctor tells you, Danny. If you try to leave here, now, you might not be covered, later, if something goes wrong this weekend."

I shifted my eyes back to the doctor, then my eyes darted desperately from Chief Neville to Captain Walker to Chief Jenkins, before they rested upon the clean-shaven doctor again. I exhaled. "Alright, alright. I'm here for the weekend. God, I can't believe this is happening to me." I threw the back of my head against my pillow in a display of misery.

The doctor nodded his head. "Good. I'll probably not be the one performing your cath on Monday. I think Dr. Guttimann will be here. He's very good. Nothing to worry about, okay?"

"Okay," I said. "Ohhh—Kaaay."

"Try to get some rest."

"In a hospital?" I said, facetiously. "You've got to be kidding me."

Chief Jenkins placed her left hand on my right forearm. "Relax, Danny. The weekend will go by fast."

"Okay, okay, okay," I said, exaggerating my defeat, as the doctor began to leave. I forced myself to be nice. "Thanks, Doc."

"We'll see you on Monday," he said, before he disappeared behind the curtain.

My attention darted from Chief Jenkins to Neville to Leon, then back to Jenkins again. "This is a fine mess you've got me into."

I closed my eyes and listened to them laugh.

I longed to be back at the fire station to appreciate the mundane duties of any day. Any day.

8

SCHOOL INSPECTIONS

THE MORNING HAD GROWN hot by the time the tow truck arrived and hauled away the destRiced vehicle.

Stripped of our turnout coats and helmets, we repacked our hoseline and gathered our tools. Then Ric and I helped Sam back the engine off of Chesapeake Boulevard onto Sheppard Avenue, by watching for and directing traffic, before we climbed into the engine's passenger compartment, which was an enclosed cab designed to accommodate up to four tailboard fire fighters in the rear and house the captain and the driver in front. There was full communication between the rear and front sections of the cab's compartment, as well as weather protection for everybody—particularly, the tailboard fire fighters at Station Fifteen, who until recently were riding in open jump seats behind the enclosed cab of an old fire engine.

Sam turned off the emergency running lights. "Everybody ready?"

"Let's go," said Ric.

Sam eased the engine onto Chesapeake Boulevard and, after he turned left onto Fishermans Road, I knew we were going to use the hydrant in front of our station to top off our engine's tank.

I relaxed into my jump seat. "What are you planning for us today, Cookie?"

Ric shook his head. "Hell, I don't know. What do you want?"

"I don't know. Anything you make is fine with me."

"What do you want, Sam?" he shouted.

"You're the cook," said Sam.

"What about you, Captain?"

"I'll eat anything you put on the table."

"Except liver," Ric amended

"Except liver."

"And tuna fish," said the captain.

"No tuna."

"And—"

"What about burgers on the grill?" Sam suggested.

"That suits me fine," said Ric. He looked at me.

"Works for me."

"Tater-tots or chips?"

"Chips," I said. "Let's keep the galley cool today."

"Besides, we have school inspections this morning," said Ron, our captain.

"Alright. Chips it is. That takes care of lunch. I'll see about dinner after we get to the store."

Ric and I popped open our side-doors and jumped out as soon as the engine stopped at the hydrant in front of the station. He went to the rear of the engine to get the hydrant wrench and I went to the left side compartment to get the fill-hose. By the time I got to the hydrant, Ric had unscrewed the hydrant cap and Sam had removed the intake cap and dropped the tank in order to take on water. The captain was standing by with his portable radio waiting for us to finish so he could clear us from the incident and place us back into commission.

I unrolled the short fill-hose toward Sam and guided the female coupling to the hydrant, while Sam guided the male coupling to the engine's intake. As soon as both couplings were tightened into place, I heard Ric say, "Ready?"

Sam nodded. "Water."

Ric opened the fire hydrant with the wrench as Sam opened the intake valve to receive the water. The short line jerked and expanded and stiffened into a tight arc, which caused a right-angle kink that I straightened out by dragging the line into a wider arc.

"Which school are we doin' first?" Sam asked.

"Bay View," said Ron.

"Alright."

The engine's tank overflowed.

Sam closed off the intake valve as Ric shut down the hydrant. As soon as the line slackened, I unhooked the fill-hose at the female hydrant end and Sam unhooked the fill-hose at the male intake end. Then I rolled up the fill-hose while Ric capped the hydrant and Sam capped the intake.

"Are we ready to go back into commission?" the captain asked.

"We're ready," Sam said.

"Do it," Ric added, as he mounted the hydrant wrench back into the slot at the rear of the engine.

"Yeah. We're done," I said, as I stowed the fill-hose back into the side compartment and pulled the door closed.

The captain keyed his portable radio. "Engine Fifteen, dispatcher."

"Dispatcher, go ahead, Fifteen."

"Engine Fifteen's in the clear and in quarters."

"Ten-four, Engine Fifteen." There was a pause. "Engine Fifteen's in the clear at 0843. Run number: 1048."

"Ten-four." The captain wrote down the time and the incident number in his pocket-pad, then he went into his office.

After Ric and I stepped into the street to stop the flow of traffic, Sam drove the engine diagonally across the center of the street and backed the engine into the station's front apron. Ric and I followed the engine onto the apron and opened our jump seat doors to retrieve our shoes. Then we took off our turnout pants and boots, slipped on our shoes, threw our turnout gear in the compartment, and double-checked our jump seats to make sure our equipment was ready to go for the next run.

Ric stretched his arms and back. "Reckon we got time for another cup of coffee?"

"Of course," I said.

I went to the large bathroom, located between the barracks bedroom and the locker room, to wash my hands and face. Ric went to the smaller bathroom located in the watchroom next to the galley.

Before we converged in the galley for a quick cup of coffee, Ric checked the galley cupboards and made a list of required food supplies that he needed for today's meals, the captain dashed out a fire report and located his schools inspection notebook, and Sam and I checked off the engine inventories as well as put out the trash.

Ron slid his empty coffee cup away from him and got up from the table. "Are we ready?"

"Reckon so," said Ric.

We migrated into the empty apparatus floor.

"Let's get these schools done before something else happens," I said.

As we ambled out to the engine, the captain pressed the switch to close the overhead apparatus door. Sam started the engine as soon as he climbed into the cab and made sure we were all onboard before he released the parking brakes and shifted into gear. He made a left on Fishermans Road, an immediate right on Sturgis Road, and approached Bay View School, which was across the intersection of Bay View Boulevard.

Sam made a right on Bay View, then parked the engine across the street from the school. Ric and I and the captain climbed out of the piece; Sam remained in the cab.

These routine school inspections were dull and the captain didn't like spending too much time doing them. We entered the main office glowing with public relations smiles and encountered the usual crestfallen expressions from the office staff.

"Please, not a fire drill today." The lady, who was the assistant school principal according to her desk nameplate, reached into her middle desk drawer for their fire drill logbook.

"Not if you've had one lately," the captain said politely.

"We had one the day before yesterday," she said, as she approached the main counter with the logbook, opened it to the proper page, and laid it on the counter in his direction.

"The day before yesterday. That's good." Ron leaned over the logbook and read the entries. "The drill time is good. The number of students has remained the same?"

"Yes."

"Isn't it a beautiful day today?" The captain dated and signed the logbook.

"Yes." She smiled. "It's lovely. But I fear it's already getting too hot out there."

"I believe you're right, ma'am." The captain wrote down the school's present occupancy and the date of their last fire drill and closed the logbook. "Have a nice day."

The lady's face brightened. "No fire drill?"

"You had one the day before yesterday. No reason to have another."

"Wonderful," she said.

"There was an exit sign that needed fixing the last time we were here."

"Ohhh, we took care of that. It's shining brightly as we speak."

"Good, good. Well, have a nice day."

"You, too."

The lady took the logbook back to her desk as we waved to the other ladies in the office and shuffled out into the main hallway.

"You sure we don't need to check nothin'?" said Ric.

Ron shook his head. "Nah. Not this time. Let's knock out the other two schools so we can get to the store."

"I'm for that," said Ric.

We went out through the main doorway and headed for the engine when we saw a two-door sedan weaving toward the engine from the north side of Sturgis Road. The vehicle jumped the curb onto the Bay View School's front lawn, swerved toward us, and stopped.

Ric's eyes widened, then he looked at me. "What have we got here?"

I shrugged my shoulders and looked at Ron. "I think we're about to find out."

"Let's go see."

Sam jumped out of the engine's cab to join us.

9

DELIVERING A BABY

As we approached the vehicle, a hysterical man on the driver's side and an equally distraught woman on the passenger's side flung their doors open and got out of the car. They stumbled across the lawn toward us, shouting and waving and pointing at their car.

I ran to the driver's side of the vehicle and Ric went to the passenger's side, while the captain approached the couple. I heard something about their teenage daughter in the back seat. Stomach pains. Hurry. She's in pain.

As soon as I pulled the front seat forward and looked down at the young girl lying in the back seat, her water broke. "Oh, my God." I stepped inside and knelt beside her.

"What!" said Ric, as he pulled forward the seat on his side.

"She's having a baby."

"Damn!"

"Give me a pair of scissors. Hurry!"

Ric dashed outside and hollered at Sam, who was approaching them. "Medical bag. Obstetrics! Scissors! Hurry!"

Without question, Sam turned around and ran back to the engine to get what was needed. And without delay, the captain keyed his portable radio to call the dispatcher and request a rescue unit and a zone car to the scene. Amid the girl's screams, I heard the captain transmit, "Delivery in progress."

When I unbuttoned and unzipped the girl's tight jeans, her belly expanded like a balloon. She squirmed and hollered and thrashed her head from side to side as I tried to stay calm. A million years went by before Ric reappeared with the partially opened emergency delivery pack; Sam extended a pair of surgical scissors through the open door behind me.

"Looks like this girl ain't waitin'," Ric said.

"You've got that right. Give that delivery pack to Sam and get in here." I guided the scissors to the right cuff of her jeans and cut along the side of her leg to her waist as Ric tried to reassure the young lady. Then I went up the left leg with the scissors. When I pulled the cut jeans aside, I saw that the baby was crowning. The only thing that was holding the baby inside her was the crotch of the girl's underpants. "Ric, come closer. Get ready to catch this baby."

Ric wedged alongside me as I carefully slipped the bottom cutting edge of the scissors underneath the young lady's underpants above the baby's crown.

"Are you ready?"

"I guess."

I snipped the crotch, and the baby shot out of the girl into Ric's awaiting hands. The girl stopped screaming, then collapsed with relief and exhaustion.

Ric and I looked at each other, then the baby, then the young lady, in a moment of shock.

The captain poked his head through the passenger's side-door and leaned over the front seat. "Is everything alright in here?"

"The baby's delivered," I said. "Where's that rescue unit?"

"Damn." Ron backed out of the vehicle's interior and keyed his portable radio. "Engine Fifteen, dispatcher."

"Dispatcher, go ahead."

"I need an ETA on that rescue unit and zone car. Baby has been delivered. I repeat. Baby has been delivered."

"She ain't breathin' too good," said Sam, as he handed Ric a small rubber syringe from the opened emergency delivery pack.

Ric inserted the rubber syringe inside the baby's mouth to suction the fluid. "Damn, I need more room. I need to get her outside."

Sam handed me two clamps. "Tie her off and cut the umbilical."

"Right."

Ric suctioned the baby's nostrils as I clamped off the umbilical. As soon as I cut the cord, Ric took the infant outside and began rubbing the baby's back to encourage her to breathe.

The captain approached Ric. "How is she doing?"

"Don't know, yet."

Sam climbed into the back seat with the remainder of the delivery kit to help me with the young lady. She was exhausted, but calm.

"She ain't bleedin' too much," Sam said, as he handed me a set of sterile gloves and several sanitary napkins.

I gloved up. "Thanks." Then I took the napkins and gently wiped some of the blood from her vaginal opening.

"Here you go." Sam handed me a couple of towels after I discarded the napkins. "One underneath her and one on top."

I took one towel and tucked it under her buttocks, then I draped the other towel over her vaginal area. I heard sirens in the distance.

"I thought we were on school inspections," I said.

Sam grunted. "Looks like we're havin' a day."

I grunted back. "You've got that right. How's the baby doing, Ric?"

"She's breathing," said the captain.

"And she's got a pulse," Ric added.

Two rescue units and a zone car finally converged upon us. They packaged the baby in one unit and the young mother in the other, and left us with the stunned parents.

"Where are they taking my girl?" the father asked.

"To Norfolk General," said the captain.

"The school nurse told us she had a stomach ache," the mother said.

The father shook his head in disbelief. "Pregnant. I didn't know my baby girl was pregnant. She's only fifteen years old."

We listened. We remained silent. And we shrugged sympathetically as the captain got their names and addresses for his fire report, then cautioned them to be careful driving to the emergency room.

After we cleared the scene, the captain decided to cancel the rest of the school inspections.

Sam remained quiet as he drove us to the store. The captain stared blankly at the road ahead. Ric complained about lunch running late.

We were emotionally exhausted.

10

PAY THE COOK

I LEANED BACK IN MY jump seat, looked out the side-door window from behind a pair of sunglasses, and attempted to emotionally disengage the aftereffects of a child having a child in the back seat of a car. I managed to flatten my dismay by the time Sam drove the engine into the parking lot of the Food Lion and position the piece so we could readily respond to our next call. Ric and I grabbed our portable radios, opened our side-doors, and climbed out of the piece as soon as we heard Sam apply the parking brakes.

I walked to the front of the engine as I turned on my radio and made sure it was set on channel one.

"Pay the cook," Ric demanded, as he approached the front of the piece from his side.

I took out six singles from my wallet and handed the bills to him.

"Pay the cook," Ric repeated, as he watched Sam and the captain climb down from the cab.

"I hope you don't burn the hamburgers this time," Sam said, as he handed Ric a twenty.

"Don't start," Ric retorted.

The captain grinned as he slid his portable radio into his back pocket. "I don't know, Sam. I kind of like charcoal in a bun."

Ric snatched the money from the captain's hand. "Pay the cook. I'll give you change later." He grimaced at Sam. "Both of you."

Sam grinned as he adjusted the volume on his radio, then slipped it into his back pocket.

"Come on, Ric." I started walking toward the grocery store. "Don't listen to them."

"I'm not! I'm not listenin'." Ric turned away from their chafing laughter and joined me.

"Yeah, you are," I said. "Your face is scrunched up like a toad."

"Not anymore." Ric displayed the cash in his hand. "I've got their money."

"Oh, Lord, look out," said Sam, as he and the captain started following us toward the grocery store's entrance.

"I reckon we're gettin' potted meat for dinner tonight," the captain added.

"I ain't listenin' to you all this mornin', I swear." Ric shoved the wad of money into his right trouser pocket.

They giggled.

I grinned, then winked at Sam as I wrapped my arm over Ric's shoulders in a display of affection. "Don't be so temperamental."

"I ain't goin' to cook no more if you all keep this up."

"Do we get our six dollars back?" Sam taunted.

Ric grinned. "Screw you."

"Ouch. You hear that, Captain?"

We laughed.

Ric grabbed an abandoned grocery cart near the electric sliding glass door and wheeled it into the air-conditioned store. I followed Ric to the meat counter in the back of the store, while Sam and the captain veered toward the bakery to get their usual morning donuts.

11

KITCHEN FIRE

"Look," I said, "they've got a special on chicken."

"I had chicken last night," said Ric.

"Ahh."

"These London Broils don't look bad." But when Ric leaned into the counter to reach for one of the meat packages in the back of the refrigerator case, our portable radios toned-out.

"That's us!" Sam hollered from the other end of an aisle running perpendicularly to the meat counter section that Ric and I were standing at.

Sam always kept his radio on channel two, the paramedical channel, instead of channel one, the fire channel, because the dispatchers always toned-out channel two before channel one. We never understood the logic behind this procedure since the engine's required three-minute response time always placed the engine on the scene before any rescue unit; engines were expected to arrive on the scene first.

Ric and I abandoned the grocery cart and charged down the aisle toward the front of the store with the volume of our radios turned up to listen to the specifics of the forthcoming dispatch.

"Ten-one apartment fire. Engine Fifteen respond to 1701 Little Creek Road, Apartment Two, at Pinewood Apartments. Time out: 1028."

We increased our charge into a full run as we heard the captain key his radio. "Engine Fifteen's responding."

"Ten-four, Engine Fifteen."

"Damn, that's close," Ric mumbled.

"We could almost walk there."

"Sure enough."

The engine was idling and the emergency lights were flashing by the time we climbed onboard. Sam released the parking brake and stepped on the accelerator as soon as he heard our side-doors slam shut and heard Ric shout, "We're in! Let's go!"

Sam took a careful right turn in the parking lot as I kicked off my shoes, stepped into my turnout boots, and pulled my night-pants up to my waist. Then Sam made a careful left turn onto Little Creek Road as I pulled my suspenders over my shoulders, struggled into my turnout coat as I maintained my balance, pulled my Nomex hood past my head and down around my neck, buttoned my coat, and opened the cylinder valve on my SCBA tank before sitting in my jump seat and inserting my arms through the harness straps.

"I see smoke," the captain said. "Looks like we got one."

Ric and I glanced at each other.

I snugged down my shoulder straps, buckled and tightened my waist strap, and draped my mask harnesses over my neck. At this point, I liked to check the air flow in my SCBA. I lifted the facepiece to my ear and cracked open the mainline valve on my regulator, which was attached to my waist strap.

Air flowed.

I shut the valve, dropped the mask, inserted my portable radio into my left turnout coat pocket, hooked a smoke cutter to my left shoulder strap, put on my helmet and tightened the chin-strap, and pulled out my gloves from my right turnout coat pocket and slipped them on. Then I squirmed in my jump seat to make sure my SCBA harness straps were tight.

Ric pulled his tank out of its jump seat cradle, stood up, and turned around to see what lay ahead. "She's lit off, alright."

I pulled my own tank from its jump seat cradle and stood up. When I turned around, I saw heavy smoke. "It's on my side."

"Damn, you!"

Ric and I always competed for the nozzle. He was an aggressive fire fighter, and I always had to move quickly to steal the nozzle from him.

As Sam drove up to the front of the building, the captain went on the air.

"Engine Fifteen's on the scene. We have a two-story, multiple-dwelling, frame structure, with heavy smoke showing. Engine Fifteen's in command."

"Ten-four, Engine Fifteen."

"Engine Fifteen, to Engine Sixteen."

"Engine Sixteen, go ahead."

"Bring in a hydrant."

"Ten-four."

"Engine Fifteen, dispatcher."

"Dispatcher, go ahead."

"Send an additional engine."

"Ten-four, Engine Fifteen."

Engine Sixteen, Engine Fourteen, Ladder Fourteen, Squad Two, Battalion Two, and Rescue Sixteen were en route.

The engine stopped; we were there. The parking air-brakes hissed; we were in it. All four engine doors were snapped open; we saw people everywhere.

I lifted the nozzle from the cradle on my side, Ric grabbed a set of irons from the rear bulkhead of the jump seat compartment,

Sam engaged the engine's pump gear, and the captain continued to direct incoming units as he climbed out of the piece.

I hooked my right arm through the hose loops, pulled part of the hose section over my right shoulder, and approached the apartment building, looking for the right door to enter as Ric provided me with slack by pulling more hose off the engine's hosebed.

A lady approached me and pointed to an open door on the first floor. "In there!" she shouted. "In the kitchen!"

"Is everybody out?" I asked, as I ran past her.

"Yes! Everybody's out!"

When I reached the door, I dumped the hose from my shoulder, knelt down beside the door, and lay the nozzle on the ground. Ric hustled over to me as I pulled off my gloves and placed them on top of the nozzle.

"Everybody's out," I said, as I began to tank up.

"I heard."

I loosened my chin-strap and pushed back my helmet so it hung by the chin-strap around my neck. Then I grabbed my face-mask and lifted the rubber web over my head as I held the mask against my face. The top three straps were preadjusted, so I tightened the two bottom straps, then turned on my air. I took a deep breath.

I raised my Nomex hood over my head and adjusted its opening around the oval edge of my facepiece, raised and Velcroed my turnout coat collar, lifted my helmet from behind and screwed it on, and pulled my chin-strap tight. I slipped on my gloves, before I picked up the nozzle, then I stood up and turned to Ric, knowing he would be ready to go in.

"Ready!?"

"Let's go!"

The hoseline tightened with water.

I cracked open the nozzle, bled the air from the line, and adjusted the nozzle to a medium fog pattern. With Ric as my backup, I crouched in front of the entrance to look inside, then straightened up and walked into the hot, black smoke.

I saw an orange glow. After several steps, I opened the nozzle and directed the firestream at the glow as Ric helped me advance the line by providing me with plenty of slack.

The small kitchen was fully involved and I had to stand fast against the heat and flames until I finally knocked down the fire. As soon as everything blackened, I shut down the line and waited.

"Good one!" Ric hollered through his facemask, which muffled his voice.

"What have we got!?" the captain shouted indistinctly through his facepiece, as he stood somewhere behind us in the smoke-filled apartment.

I cracked my mask away from my face so the captain could hear me more clearly. Air escaped through the opening of my positive pressure SCBA as I spoke. "Fire is out! Fire is out, Captain!"

"Fire is out!?"

"Fire! Out!"

The captain cracked his mask away from his face before keying the radio. "Engine Fifteen, to Battalion Chief."

"Battalion Chief—go ahead, Ron."

"Fire is under control, Chief."

"Ten-four. Start ventilating the apartment. I'll have Ladder Fourteen bring in a couple of fans."

"Ten-four."

12

THE SAFETY OFFICER

WHEN I OPENED MY EYES, Captain Walker was the only person standing by my emergency room bed.

"Hey, Leon. What's going on?"

"You nodded off."

"Where's Chief Jenkins?"

"She had to go. That fire alarm turned out to be another working fire in her district."

"What a crazy night. Neville go with her?"

"He went somewhere. I don't know."

"What are you doing? Why are you still here?"

"Just making sure you're alright."

"You need to be out there being the safety officer."

"I need to be making sure your paper work is in order before I leave."

"Is it?"

He sucked on his teeth. "Yes."

I squirmed in my bed to get comfortable. "Damn. I still can't believe this is happening to me."

"Try to stop worrying about that, Danny. There's nothing you can do about it."

"I know, I know. It's just—" My mind went blank.

"Are you alright?"

I saw concern registered in Leon's face. I felt helpless. "It's as if someone turned off a switch inside of me. I feel weak and empty. It feels like all my energy and power have been drained from me."

Leon pursed his lips. "Would you like something to read? A newspaper?"

"No thanks. Besides, I can't read without my glasses."

"I have a pair you can have."

"No, no, I can't do that."

He reached into his top pocket and pulled out a pair of black steel-rimmed glasses. "Here, take these."

"I can't take your glasses."

"They're cheapos. I think I paid three dollars for them at the Dollar Store. I've got a bunch of them. Go on, take 'em." He pressed them into my left hand.

"Thanks, Leon. I can't read a thing without them. There's no telling what kind of additional forms these people are going to have me sign. I'll get them back to you."

"Just keep 'em."

"Thanks, Leon. Thanks." I closed my eyes and drifted.

13

SALVAGE AND OVERHAUL

I STOOD BY WITH the nozzle as Ric searched for windows to open in order to ventilate the room. The ladder company and the backup engine companies were already crowding into the apartment to conduct salvage and overhaul.

I heard Ric grunt as he tried to open a window. Then I heard the sound of glass breaking. The closed window must have been stuck.

Heavy black smoke forced us to work as blind men.

I heard more glass breaking, more radios blaring, and a growing concatenation of muffled voices inside the apartment. I heard fire fighters crash against and stumble over furniture. I heard crashing in another room.

I saw a piece of light, when the smoke began to clear, and realized that that must have been the window Ric smashed open. Then I saw the damage caused by the fire and the water, and the continued damage caused by the fire fighters engaged in the necessary overhaul operations as the smoke continued to clear. I saw an innocent flower vase topple from a shelf. I watched a porcelain figure become a small casualty.

I stepped aside to allow my captain and Ric and a couple of fire fighters to enter the kitchen. One fire fighter had a pick-head axe and a bucket light; the other had a pike pole and an ordinary

smoke cutter. The captain directed the light beam of his smoke cutter toward the ceiling above the stove and directed the fire fighter
with the pike pole to pull down the overhead.

The fire fighter raised the point of the six-foot pike pole close to
the ceiling, then stabbed the drywall with enough force to push the
point and its adjacent hook through the ceiling. He stepped back,
angling the end of the pike pole toward him, and pulled down on
the pole. Part of the kitchen's ceiling and insulation came down.
The fire fighter repeated this task until the floor joists supporting
the above apartment were exposed. Then the other fire fighter was
directed to chop a hole into the wall near the stove.

I stood by with the nozzle, ready to apply water to any uncovered fire extensions and smoldering debris. This was an easy job
during the early bull-labor stages of an overhaul and one of the
perks of being the first-in nozzle man.

The bell of my SCBA began to ring, indicating that I had three
to five minutes of air left. So I handed the nozzle to one of the
nearby fire fighters, even though the smoke had cleared; I knew
the forbidding atmosphere was filled with toxic gases and decided
not to take off my mask and remain inside the apartment. When I
heard Ric's bell begin to ring, as well, I informed the captain that
we were going outside.

The captain acknowledged our intended departure, then continued to direct the overhaul. Since he didn't have to carry any line
into this fire, he had a few more minutes of air left in his tank due
to less physical exertion.

When we reached the front door, we had to maneuver around
the forced draft fan installed by the ladder company.

Once outside, I pushed my helmet off my head, pulled my
Nomex hood down to my neck, and yanked off my facemask. Air
rushed out of my detached facepiece as I turned off the mainline

valve on my regulator. I placed my helmet back on my head and let the mask dangle from its neck harness in front of me.

The parking lot and the streets were littered with fire trucks and personnel, hoselines and equipment, evacuated residents and curious bystanders, police officers and paramedics. The late morning sun was bright and hot.

"Good stop," said Ric.

"I think we had it knocked down before second-in engine arrived on the scene."

"Yeah. We kicked butt on this one. I think I'll rag the boys on Engine Sixteen for takin' so long to get here."

I chuckled. "Those boys will love you for that." I felt good. I liked the feeling of making this job appear easy. I liked aggressive fire attacks. And I liked the comradery and the professional competition between fire companies.

We stopped by our engine before going to the squad truck.

"Thanks for the water, Sam," I said.

"Alright."

Ric took off his helmet. "We had us a good one."

"You all want to change tanks?"

"Naw," said Ric. "We'll get these jammed at the squad while we're takin' our break."

"Damn, if we ain't havin' us a day," said Sam.

"It's another great fire department day!"

Sam chuckled at my ridiculously joyful remark. Ric complained about lunch.

"The hell with making lunch," I said.

"You've got that right." Ric relaxed. "How about McDonald's hamburgers?"

"Don't matter to me. Sam?"

"I don't care."

"Come on, Ric. Let's top off our tanks."

We sauntered over to the squad truck and approached the driver-operator, who was standing by the raised rear door of the piece.

"Hey there, Hernandez. What's your no good?" said Ric.

"Same ol', same ol'."

I turned my back to Hernandez and leaned forward. "Top us off, big boy."

Hernandez reached for my cylinder valve and shut off my tank. "Bleed it down."

I cracked open my regulator's mainline valve and released the trapped air.

Hernandez unscrewed the high pressure line from my tank. "Anything to it in there?"

"Naw," said Ric. "Just a nice little fun fire."

"A quick stop," I added. "Went right to it. Textbook."

Hernandez released the clamp that loosened the aluminum strap around the cylinder, then pulled the tank out of my shoulder harness. "Those are nice, when you can get 'em."

"Yeah."

Hernandez laid my tank on the bed of the squad truck and directed Ric to turn around.

I unhooked my facemask's harness from around my neck, took off my helmet, and dropped both articles on the ground. Then I sat down on the rear bumper and watched Hernandez remove Ric's tank from his shoulder harness. "Now that you've got a driver's job, Hernandez, how do you like permanent squad work?"

"It's alright, I guess. But I never get a chance to be first-in anymore."

"That's too bad."

"Shoot, I don't think I'd like that," said Ric, as he removed his Nomex hood from around his neck.

"Yeah," I added, "that—and having to drive this breadbox all over the city—"

"Screw you," said Hernandez.

"Ouch. You hear that, Ric?"

"Ah, huh." Ric pretended he was bewildered. "He hurt my feelin's, too."

"Bite me. Both of you."

"Stick it out here," Ric taunted. "Come on. I'll bite it."

Hernandez chuckled as he attached Ric's tank to the recharging line of the squad truck's cascade system. "There's cold water in the back of the chief's van."

"Thanks, bud." Ric sat next to me on the rear bumper and exhaled.

We stared into the distance and enjoyed our break.

14

ROOM 225

I OPENED MY EYES and saw Leon stepping aside for a nurse and an orderly.

"Did I drift off again, Leon?"

"They're taking you to your room."

"Ah." I looked at the orderly.

"Enjoy the ride," he said, as the nurse disconnected me from the heart monitor.

As soon as Leon's radio toned-out, he lowered the volume. "I've got to go, Danny."

"I know. Thanks for staying around for as long as you have."

"Call me if you need anything. Anything."

"Right. I will. Thanks."

The nurse removed the blood pressure cuff from my left arm.

"You sure you don't want me to call Kathleen for you?"

"Naw. I'll . . . I'll call her later this morning."

"Okay. I'll drop in on you."

"Anytime. I'll be here partying all weekend."

Leon chuckled, then disappeared behind the surrounding curtains.

"You don't need this IV anymore," said the nurse, as she pulled the tape, which held the needle in place, from the back of my hand.

"Oww."

"Sorry."

"Gee, I hate to lose my hair that way."

Her eyes brightened. She pulled out the needle and discarded it. "I'm going to have to insert a saline-lock. Do you want it on the right or the left hand?"

"Let's stay with the left hand, if that's alright."

"Left hand it is." She opened a sterile package containing a needle and another package containing a short piece of intravenous tubing with a plastic nipple at one end and a rubber appliance at the other end. She swabbed the back of my hand with an alcohol pad, inserted the needle into a vein, and pulled out a plastic device that ran the length of the needle. Then she deftly plugged the supply end of the needle with the plastic nipple. After she taped the needle and the looped intravenous tubing to the back of my hand, she inserted the blunt end of a plastic plunger into the rubber appliance and shot a syringeful of saline solution into my vein to clear my blood from the saline-lock. "There. You're ready to go."

"Thanks." I looked at the orderly. "Drop me off at the nearest pub."

"Sorry. Last call was a couple of hours ago." The orderly pulled two of the surrounding curtains open, released the bed's brake, and guided my bed onto the emergency room's main floor where the lights were brighter. We went for a ride through a maze of rooms and hallways and electric doors to get to an elevator that took us to the second floor. Then we traveled through more hallways and doors until we reached room 225, a semiprivate room with another patient already occupying the window side of the room.

A nurse entered the room as the orderly wheeled my bed into place, engaged the brake, and left without acknowledging me.

"I'm Clorisa," the nurse said. "How do you feel?"

"Tired. Miserable. I want to go home."

"I know." Then she attached the numerous leads to a portable heart monitor, the size of a transistor radio, to the round patches that were still taped to my chest. "We'll get you home soon."

"Sure, sure. I bet you say that to all your patients."

She smiled. Took my temperature, pulse, and blood pressure. Checked my saline-lock. Then she gave me a pair of open-backed pajamas to put on.

"Oh, boy. Can I wear the ties in front?"

"That would be a very revealing fashion statement," she said.

"Not so good, huh?"

"Not unless you want to be embarrassed all weekend."

"Right." I believe she was genuinely amused with me.

She helped me out of my bed and guided me into the bathroom. And while I changed into the hospital pajamas, she placed a large Styrofoam cup of water with a plastic straw impaled through its plastic lid on my bedside table along with a set of towels and a bag of toiletries. Then she helped me back into my bed and hung my clothes in the closet beside my bed.

"I'm cold."

She brought me a blanket, spread it over my sheet, demonstrated how to use the call button, and promised to look in on me later. Then she pulled the hospital room's door closed and left me in semidarkness.

I closed my eyes to explore my own darkness. But I drifted, and simply exchanged one kind of darkness for another.

15

THE FIREGROUND

RIC AND I DITCHED our tanks near our piece to lighten our loads before we sauntered back into the apartment from our break.

Sunlight invaded the soot-covered interior through broken windows, which created sorry shadows and highlighted the damage and debris in the dark surroundings. The atmosphere was tolerably clear of residual smoke and toxic fumes.

"Hey, Captain, what's goin' on?"

"Nothing much, Ric. I think we've got it. Do me a favor and double-check these walls and ceilings before the chief starts clearing companies."

"Where's the chief?" I asked.

"She went back to her car. Good job, you all."

"I guess we did alright," Ric said.

"At least, that's what Chief Jenkins thinks."

"Oww! Captain, that hurt," said Ric.

I laughed. Ric smirked.

Ron responded to me with a mischievous grin. "I keep forgetting how delicate he is."

I thumped Ric's chest. "No thick skin here." Then I pretended to pull out an arrow from his chest. "See?"

"Lord, God, you two are—"

"Come on, you fool. Let's finish this job so we can get out of here."

Ric inspected the torn-out walls in the kitchen with his smoke cutter, while I climbed the combination ladder and poked my head between the floor joists to check for hidden hot spots with my smoke cutter.

"It looks clear up here," I said to Ron, as I continued to scan the ceiling.

"It looks clear down here, too," Ric added, a few moments later.

Chief Jenkins entered the apartment. "I'd like to start clearing more companies, Ron. I just let Fourteen go."

"That's fine, Chief. Good. I think you can let everybody go but us."

The ladder company started disconnecting the power from the fans as soon as they overheard Ron's recommendation.

"Don't you want to keep the ladder a little while longer?"

"No, Chief. They're done. They can clear up."

"Okay."

I lowered my head below the ceiling joists without taking a step down the ladder. "Hey, Chief! How's everything going?"

She peered up to me. "I'm doing fine, Danny. Good job—you and Ric."

"Thanks, Mother Tasha."

She responded jubilantly to Ric's address. "I swear, I miss being the captain at Fifteen."

"You can't have them back," said Ron.

"I know, I know."

"You'll just have to enjoy us when you can," I said.

She glowed with a broad grin. "Alright, Ron, I'm clearing everybody but Engine Fifteen."

I climbed down from the ladder after Chief Jenkins left the apartment and approached the captain. "If it's alright with you, Ric and I are going to have Sam shut down the line so we can pack hose."

"Go ahead. As soon as Arson gets here to investigate, we're clearing."

"Okay."

I heard the chief go on the air from my portable radio:

"Battalion Two, dispatcher."

"Dispatcher, go ahead."

"Clear all units with the exception of Engine Fifteen."

"Ten-four, Battalion Two." My radio toned-out. "Clearing all units at 1701 Little Creek Road, with the exception of Engine Fifteen."

I grabbed the nozzle on my way out of the apartment and Ric got hold of the line about half a section behind me. We dragged the hose out of the apartment as Squad Two, Rescue Sixteen, and Battalion Two were driving away. The boys on Ladder Fourteen were stowing the ventilation fans and coiling the extension cords, and the boys on Engine Sixteen were packing the five-inch line they laid from the hydrant to our engine.

As soon as I caught Sam's attention, I pressed my straightened fingers together and simulated cutting my throat. "Shut her down!" I hollered unnecessarily.

I waited for Sam to reduce the pressure and shut down the line before I opened the nozzle to release the water from the inch-and-three-quarters hoseline. Then Ric and I broke the fifty-foot sections at their couplings while Sam climbed into the cab to take the engine out of pump gear.

Each of us filled in the holes; that is, each of us constantly found the task opposite to the task already taken to get the job done. Filling in these holes on the fireground was like a dance among working men. The veteran fire fighter who understood this was considered a good fireground man and the veteran who didn't was considered a load. A rookie who didn't understand was expected to learn from a veteran, and a rookie who managed to stay busy, because he saw the holes, was considered a natural.

By the time Ric and I had all six sections of hose disconnected, Sam had remounted our hand tools and SCBA equipment and had the engine's intake and supply openings capped. Then he helped us straighten out the broken sections, drain the water from each line, roll up the dirty front two sections and stow them into our jump seat compartment, and repack the four remaining sections into our crosslay hosebed.

When we were done, I looked at Engine Sixteen to assess that company's progress. They had finished draining their five-inch with their hose roller and were preparing to pack the rear hosebed.

"Let's give those boys a hand," Sam said, as soon as I looked at him.

I nodded. "Come on."

Ric wasted no time in joining us to assist Engine Sixteen with their five-inch.

We were filling in the hole as an engine company.

16

KEVIN BROOKE

"Hey, Dana. Dana. Are you awake?"

I opened my eyes and saw a man, wearing a hospital gown, standing at my bedside. Although it was still dark, I could see that he was about my age and stature.

"I was asleep," I said irritably.

"You were? Damn, Dana, shape up. We've gotta break out of this joint."

"I'm not Dana."

"What?" The guy leaned close to my face and squinted.

"My name's Danny," I said.

"Whoa! Where have you been, Danny? I've been waiting for you all night."

I repositioned my portable heart monitor with my right hand as I shifted onto my left side. "Well, I've been here all night."

"You have?"

"Yeah."

"Are you sure?"

"I'm sure. Go check," I said, in order to get him away from my bedside.

"Yeah. Good idea. I will." My roommate went to the hospital room's door, carefully opened it, and peered it into the hallway.

I sighed. I was obviously sharing a room with a nut. A harmless one, I hoped.

I closed my eyes and tried to fall back to sleep.

"Dana. Dana. Are you awake?"

I pressed the side of my face against my pillow. "What?"

"Dana!"

I opened my eyes. "What!"

"Are you awake?"

"I am now." My eyes adjusted to the darkness again and rested upon the nervous figure standing beside my bed. "Did you check?"

"What?"

"I've been here all night."

"Well of course you have."

I exhaled. "Oh, boy."

"What?"

"Nothing." I shifted in my bed in an attempt to get comfortable. "What's your name?"

The man's eyes widened with surprise. "Don't you recognize me? It's Kevin, man. Kevin Brooke."

"Oh. Yeah. Kevin."

"Man. Don't ever scare me like that."

I groaned.

Kevin leaned toward me. "Hey, are you alright, Dana?"

"Don't you sleep?"

"That's a dangerous occupation around here. You want a beer?"

"No."

"Come on. Let's make a break for it. There's a nice bar downstairs. I've been there many, many times."

"What bar?"

"Michael O'Grady's."

"Hospitals don't have bars."

Kevin scurried to the door, carefully cracked it open, and peered into the hallway again. "Are you sure about this, Dana?"

"My name's Danny."

"Those women don't look like nurses to me. Do you have the key?"

"What key?"

"To the door! We can't continue leaving this door unlocked."

"The door doesn't have a lock. This is a hospital."

Kevin tried to digest this information. He became worried and began to pace the floor.

"Go to bed, Kevin. Don't you sleep?"

"We've got to break out of this place, Dana."

"Let me sleep, Kevin. Okay? Please. Let me sleep."

"Sure, sure. Get some sleep. I'll have the plan ready in the morning."

"Go to your bed, Kevin."

"Sure, sure."

Kevin approached his bed with great trepidation and sat on its edge, facing me.

I wanted to close my eyes and get some sleep, but I knew it was hopeless. There was no escape. My heart attack left me weak and confined to this hospital bed and trapped with Kevin Brooke, who was suffering from God-knows-what.

17

GROCERY SHOPPING

"Ric?"

"What?"

Sam pointed at the meat counter's chicken section. "There's a special on breasts."

"I had chicken yesterday."

"What about this London Broil?" I suggested.

"Are you all goin' to let me cook or what?"

"Damn." Sam winked at me. "We're just tryin' to help."

"Help, my ass. I don't ever see you in the galley."

"Lighten up, Ric," I said, as I winked back at Sam.

"Easy for you to say. You're goin' to get yourself a nap this afternoon while I'm stuck in the galley cookin'."

I put my arm around Ric's neck and smiled at Sam. "Come on, brother. We'll help you, right, Sam?"

"Sure." Sam couldn't contain himself. "There's nothin' to burnin' meat on a grill and throwin' it on our plates."

"Alright, don't start." Ric broke away from my caress and reached into the meat counter. He brought out a large package of pork chops. "These here look good." He presented the package to me. "What do you think?"

"Looks good to me." I peered at Sam. "Pork chops?"

"On the grill?"

"With barbecue sauce," said Ric.

"Works for me."

"Corn on the cob?" I added.

"Sure."

"And cole slaw?" Sam interjected.

"Store bought," Ric cautioned. "I ain't makin' fresh."

"Store bought is fine," I said. "Make it easy on yourself."

"Don't forget the rolls," Sam said.

"I won't, I won't. Since when have I ever forgotten rolls?" Ric grimaced.

"Calm down." Sam grinned sheepishly. "Damn. Look at the scowl on that face."

I affectionately put my right arm across Ric's shoulders. "Easy there, boy. We're just trying to help."

"Not if you two keep windin' me up."

I suppressed a smile. "There's no reason for you to miss your nap this afternoon." Sam's portable radio, which was set on channel two, toned out. "That is, unless—"

"That's not us," said Sam. "It's Rescue Thirteen."

"Good." I looked at Ric as I released my embrace. "Come on, brother, let's get shopping so we can get out of here."

The three of us orbited the grocery cart as we traveled down the aisles searching for the things Ric needed. Then we found an empty register and helped the checkout lady bag our groceries. The register rang up nineteen dollars and eighty-four cents.

"Look at that," Ric said. "Everyone gets a dollar back."

"We'd have gotten back more," said Sam, "if you'd have picked a special out of that meat counter."

"Gripe, gripe, gripe. Wait 'til you taste them pork chops for dinner tonight. You'll see."

18

BREAKFAST

As I waited for my breakfast, Kevin Brooke was rummaging through the drawer of his bedside table for the sixth time. I wanted to ask him what he was searching for, but I did not want to subject myself to his response. I thwarted temptation by calling my wife. Besides, it was past eight o'clock and she would be expecting me home by now.

"Hello, hon? Hi. How are you this morning? Good. Look, sweetheart, umm . . . I don't want you to get excited, because I'm alright. Nothing's wrong. Well. I'm in the hospital. I'm okay. I had a heart attack while fighting a fire last night. Yeah. I'm at DePaul Hospital. Right. There's no reason for you to rush right over. I'm fine. I'm waiting for breakfast and all that stuff. Right. Well, I'm here for the weekend because they want to do a heart catheterization on Monday. I'm in room two-twenty-five. Can you bring me my bathrobe and that small bag with my toilet articles and, let's see—a book? Yeah. Ohhh . . . bring me, let me think. Bring me . . . T. S. Elliot's *The Complete Poems and Plays.* Yes. That should do it. It's in the bookcase behind my desk. Alright. No, that should do it. A little poetry is all I can handle right now—if that. Thanks, honey. And look, don't rush. I don't want you having an accident driving over here. Are you alright? Good. You know how to get here? It's on Granby Street, that's right. I love you, too." A lady with a tray entered the room and placed it on Kevin's bed table. "They're serving us breakfast. Oh, boy. Yeah. I'm kind of hungry, too. I'm fine. Really. You be careful. And don't rush. Love you. Bye." I hung up the telephone and waited for my tray.

Kevin sat on the edge of his bed facing me and peered over the food tray on his bed table. "Come on. Roll that table of yours on this side and join me for breakfast."

I pushed the bed table aside, sat up, grabbed a hold of my portable heart monitor, and swung my legs over the left side of my bed. By the time I tucked my heart monitor into the waistband of my boxer shorts and positioned my table in front of me, the lady was presenting me with my breakfast.

"Good morning."

"Good morning," she sang, as she set the tray on my table.

"Thank you. I hope there's scrambled eggs and sausage with a nice stack of pancakes in there."

She smiled. "You've got to know better than that."

"Can't blame a guy for trying," Kevin said. "Brother, what I wouldn't do for a stack of hot pancakes soaked with syrup."

I winked at the lady. "Go ahead. Show me my culinary surprise."

She lifted the thick plastic cover from my tray and placed it on top of Kevin's plastic cover that was resting on the seat of a straight-backed chair.

My plate looked empty. "Ouch."

"I'll be back for your tray and your menus."

"You mean I won't have to repeat this meal again?"

The lady laughed as she left the room.

I was bewildered by the stark presentation set before me. At the center of the tray was a plate with a cold, dry bagel split in half. To the upper right was a box of cereal sitting in a small bowl. To the upper left was a container of room-temperature milk and next to that a plastic tumbler of apple juice sealed with aluminum foil. In a rectangular receptacle to the left of my plate lay a set of utensils, a napkin, a small plastic tub of margarine, and a single packet of sugar. No coffee. But I was grateful to see a cup of hot water with a plastic lid over it and an individually wrapped bag of tea beside it.

Kevin leaned over his tray toward me. "This shit is not exactly from the Ritz."

I looked at his tray. He had cream cheese and jelly to spread on his bagel. There was real coffee. Scrambled eggs and grits. Orange juice and—"You're outfit looks a lot better than mine."

"Don't worry. It'll get better after they start bringing what you ordered." He pulled a piece of paper from his tray. "See this? It's tomorrow's menu."

I slid mine out from under the paper napkin and glanced at it. "I see."

"Check everything you can get on it. With luck, there'll be something on tomorrow's tray that you can eat." He saw me studying his tray. "It's still crap."

I laid the menu on my bed. "Can I have one of your jellies?"

"Sure." He tossed me a grape.

"Thanks."

"Yeah, these stale bagels are pretty dry without jelly. Yeah, in Nam, I would have killed for a jelly."

"You were in Vietnam?"

"Wasn't everybody?"

"Well—I was there."

"See?" He presented me with a can of strawberry Boost. "Cough up a nickel and you can have one of these."

"No, thanks."

Crestfallen, he looked at the can of Boost, then extended it to me. "You can have it anyway."

"That's alright, Kevin. I'm happy with the grape jelly."

Kevin set the Boost on his tray. "That's good stuff." He cracked his neck. "Just let me know if there's anything I can do for you, my man."

"Thanks, Kevin." I opened the small box of cereal and shook the contents into my bowl. Then I opened the sugar packet and sprinkled the brown flakes. I picked up my spoon, opened the container of milk, and poured half of it over my cereal. "So. How old are you, Kevin?"

He bit into his cream cheese and jelly bagel. "Twenty-four."

"Ah." I began eating my cereal.

Kevin appeared to be in his late forties, early fifties. He was partially bald and redheaded, freckle-faced and green-eyed. He had a friendly disposition.

"When were you in-country?"

Kevin stopped chewing his food in order to think. "Let's see. Ninety-eight, eighty-eight, seventy-eight, sixty-eight—that's right. In sixty-eight."

"Ah. With what outfit?"

"Army."

I unwrapped my tea bag and dropped it into my cup of warm water. "And . . . and how old are you?"

He stopped chewing, again, to think. "Let's see. Ninety-four, eighty-four, seventy-four, sixty-four—that's right. Twenty-four." He looked at his bitten bagel, which had a thick layer of cream cheese troweled across its face, and threw it on his plate. "Damn. This thing is dry. I'd rather eat C-rations."

"Yeah."

Kevin leaned across his tray and whispered. "Have you ever witnessed a murder?"

"No."

"It's one of the most disgusting things I've ever seen."

I kept eating my cereal. "What happened?"

"Well, this guy ran an ice cream parlor that served vanilla syrup."

"Ah-ha."

"And the fight was over the fact that the customer, who didn't like vanilla, was a complete asshole."

"Right. And?"

"Well, he chopped him up and put him in a vanilla fruit cake and sent the guy to South Africa." Kevin vigorously rubbed his thighs. "Damn. Turn the heat on. It's cold in here."

Our day nurse came into our room. "Hello. I'm Karen. Is everything alright?"

"I guess you can call it that," I said.

She went to the miniature white marker board that hung from a wall hook, erased the night nurse's name, and wrote hers down. "I'll be here until tonight. I'm on double shift."

"Great," said Kevin, with a tremendous display of enthusiasm. "She knows how to take care of me."

"Are you behaving, Kevin?"

Kevin feigned innocence. "I haven't done nothin'. Ask Dana."

She threw an inquiring glance at me to assess my perception, as well as my tolerance, of Kevin's mental condition.

"Kevin and I are doing alright, together," I said.

The nurse's eyes softened. "Good. Very good. I'm glad. Call me for any reason."

"Thanks," I said.

As soon as she left, Kevin sighed with relief. "She's watching us like a hawk. See? I told you we've got to break out of here."

"Yeah. Right." I drank some of my lukewarm tea and stared out the window.

19

TWENTY-ONE DAY CYCLE

"ARE WE GOING TO McDonald's for hamburgers?" Ric asked, as we walked out of the Food Lion with a plastic bag full of groceries dangling from each of our right hands.

"Shoot. I ain't hungry after them donuts we just ate." Sam glanced at me. "Are you?"

"Not after eating that giant cinnamon bun you bought me. I don't think the captain's gonna be hungry, either."

"Naw." Sam burped. "He bought three donuts and a container of chocolate milk before he went back to the piece to wait for us."

"There it is," said Ric.

"What?" I said.

"Lunch ruined."

"What in the world are you talkin' about?" said Sam.

"I can hear you all tonight in the watchroom."

"What!"

"Talkin' about how easy the cook's got it."

Sam glanced at me as he tried to suppress a grin. "Lord God, Ric, give it up. We ain't sayin' nothin'."

Ric pouted. "Not now."

I nudged Ric affectionately with my forearm as we reached the engine. "Don't worry, Ric. Like you said, your barbecued pork chops are going to be such a culinary delight this afternoon, our minds are going to go blank about lunch."

We reached the engine.

"Screw you."

I feigned innocence. "What did I say?"

Sam and I laughed as we loaded the groceries into one of the right-side compartments. Then we climbed onboard the engine.

Ric slammed shut the right jump seat door. "Are we goin' back to the station, Cap?"

"Straight back. I'm tired."

Sam started the engine. "So am I."

"Let's shut down for a while."

"Are those donuts going to hold you?" Ric asked.

"Why?"

"We figured to have an early dinner and forget lunch altogether."

"That works for me," said the captain, as Sam drove across the parking lot and stopped in front of the red traffic light leading out of the lot onto Little Creek Road. "Those donuts I ate are sittin' heavy in my stomach."

"Good."

Sam made a left turn onto Little Creek Road as soon as the traffic light turned green and headed for our station. Ric and I relaxed into our jump seats feeling pretty good.

"Damn if this mornin' didn't go by fast," said Ric.

"We've earned our money this shift," I said.

Ric looked at his watch. "All we've got left is eighteen hours."

"Shoot. Don't remind me."

"You mean you ain't got a Kelly night or somebody workin' for you?"

"Naw."

There were three shifts in the department, each working twenty-four hours while on duty. We worked in a twenty-one day cycle that averaged ten, twenty-four-hour work days a month. The cycle was constructed in the following manner: day on, day off, day on, day off, day on, day off, day on, three days off, day on, day off, day on, two days off, day on, five days off. Then the cycle started over again. A complete twenty-one-day cycle started on a Tuesday and ended on a Monday for all three shifts—A, B, and C shifts.

In an effort to keep the average work hours down to fifty-four hours a week, each fire fighter was assigned a Kelly group that subtracted a twelve-hour trick from the work cycle each month. A twelve-hour day trick off, with pay, was called a day Kelly and a twelve-hour night trick off was called a night Kelly. The day trick began at 7 A.M. and ended at 7 P.M., and the night trick started at 7 P.M. that evening and ended on the following morning at 7 A.M.

A fire fighter was also allowed to have another fire fighter work for him. These were called cash tricks. Payment was made directly from fire fighter to fire fighter, who worked on different shifts. However, if a fire fighter wished to sell his Kelly day or night, he could do so to someone on the same shift. A day trick was worth fifty dollars, a night trick fifty, and a full twenty-four was worth a hundred dollars. Since the off-going fire fighter had somebody paid to work for him, his bimonthly salary did not change; administratively, he was considered on-duty via somebody else.

"You hear that, boys?" Ric hollered. "Danny's actually spendin' twenty-four with us."

Sam and the captain chuckled.

"Don't worry," I said. "The day's young. I bet somebody in the district is already aching to sell me his Kelly night. They can't resist that fifty-dollar cash money I always have in my wallet."

Ric shook his head. "Damn. You're somethin', bud. You don't mind lettin' go of that paper."

"Life is short, bud."

"I know, I know. But I can't afford to pay to get off like you do."

"Well, I'm in training."

"Huh?"

"I'm learning how to live on half pay so, when I retire, I'll already have it figured out."

Ric chortled. "You hear that, Cap?"

"There's nothing wrong with that," said the captain.

Ric scrutinized me carefully. "I swear, you're a piece of work, Danny."

"Thank you. I aim to provide you with as much entertainment as you can handle for the next eighteen hours."

"Less twelve if you can get away with it."

"Always."

Ric shook his head and smiled.

The radio toned-out as we were approaching Chesapeake Boulevard.

"Car fire. Engine Fourteen, respond to a ten-one car fire on the 400 block of East Little Creek Road."

"That's not far from us, Captain," said Sam.

The captain unhooked the handset from the engine's dashboard and keyed the radio. "Engine Fifteen, dispatcher."

"Dispatcher, go ahead."

"We're at Little Creek Road and Chesapeake Boulevard en route to our station. We'll take that call. Go ahead and clear Engine Fourteen."

"Ten-four, Engine Fifteen."

Sam hit the lights and sirens and stepped hard on the engine's accelerator.

I kicked off my shoes, slipped my feet into my turnout boots, and pulled on my nightpants.

"I see smoke," said Ric, as he reached for his turnout coat.

"Damn," Sam uttered.

I peered over the back of my jump seat and saw several fingers of flame rising dramatically from a fully involved vehicle. "My, God." There were spectators scattered on both sides of the street.

By the time I finished buttoning my coat, we were there.

A citizen opened my jump seat door and screamed, "There's a guy burning up in that car!"

I tightened my helmet's chin-strap, lifted the nozzle off its cradle on my side, and stepped down from the piece, as another citizen frantically pointed at the burning vehicle and hollered that somebody was still in there. As I ran toward the vehicle, I laid out the inch-and-three-quarters line behind me and continued to size-up the situation.

The rear half of the vehicle was engulfed in flames. However, the fire hadn't entered the passenger's interior, yet. The heat and smoke was so intense that I knew there was a gas tank rupture feeding the fire.

I approached the driver's window and saw a man wedged between the glove compartment and the front seat. The semiconscious man squinted his bloody eyes in my direction and hollered.

I dropped the nozzle of the uncharged line to the ground, reached inside the vehicle as far as my waist, and tried to grab him. But the man's arms and shirtless body were covered with slick blood; there was broken glass everywhere.

My feet came off the ground as I slid closer to the struggling victim; Ric had a firm hold of my calves. Then I noticed that the fire was wrapping around the passenger's side of the vehicle toward the man, who began fighting with me. I realized he was probably on drugs or alcohol, or both.

I made several attempts to pull him out of the vehicle, but mere peril transformed into horror when the fire reached the victim's side of the vehicle. The man's hair lit-off with a "whoof." He screamed like a madman.

Ric helped me back out through the window.

I quickly picked up the nozzle, hoping that the broken line had been reconnected by now, but the hose was still uncharged. When I looked at Ric and saw the startled expression in his eyes, I realized he was responding to the horror that must have been registered in my eyes.

"Where's the water?" I implored.

Ric turned away from me and hollered at Sam. "Water! Give us water!"

The intense shrieks that came from the vehicle's interior were not the sounds of a human being. I ran around to the other side, where the fire was roasting the man, and felt the line tighten as soon as I was in position. I bled the line, adjusted the nozzle setting, and directed the water stream at the poor victim. He screamed.

I held the water on him until his screams abated, then I swept the fire toward the back of the vehicle.

Ric crawled inside the vehicle through the driver's window in an effort to save the victim. Two other fire fighters followed him inside to help. One of them was a rookie fire fighter called Terry Chin, who fearlessly entered the vehicle with Ric and Billy.

Because Sam had broken the line too short, I was forced to remain standing downwind of the burning vehicle and eat black smoke and toxic fumes. Also, the line was ineffective against the blaze because of a ruptured gas tank and because the single section prevented me from maneuvering behind the vehicle to flood the tank.

I wanted to back out from my position, but I was afraid that if I shut down the line and attempted to reposition myself the fire would wrap around the right side of the vehicle and burn the three fire fighters inside, who were trying to extricate the victim. I was stuck.

I alternated holding my breath with taking shallow puffs of bad air. But my heavy exertion against the fire eventually forced me to gasp deeply and take in large amounts of poisonous gas.

I held my ground. I knew this was going to cost me some of my health: probably today and most likely tomorrow and certainly during that ugly unknown year ahead when my body was ready to stay sick.

I kept the fire pushed back even though I started feeling weak and dizzy and nauseous. Then Sam dragged a charged booster line to the other side, where he was able to angle the water stream directly onto the rear of the vehicle. We managed to put the fire out just as Ric and Terry Chin and the other fire fighter extricated the screaming victim through the vehicle's window.

Several awaiting paramedics hovered around the seriously burned man and quickly packaged him into the stretcher to deliver him to an ambulance. As soon as Ric cleared the interior of the car, I shut down my nozzle. Then I coughed. I dropped the nozzle and walked away from the smoldering vehicle.

I tried to take a deep breath of fresh air, but I wheezed instead. My chest hurt. I was woozy. I coughed again and spat. A glob of black phlegm spattered on the street.

"Are you alright?"

I recognized Jason Phelps' voice, the paramedic lieutenant on the zone car, and turned around to answer him. "No."

"What's wrong?"

"I had to eat a lot of bad smoke."

He grabbed a hold of my upper left arm and guided me to his zone car. "Are you feeling dizzy?"

"Yeah. And nauseous." I looked straight into his eyes and wheezed. "I don't feel good."

He helped me out of my turnout gear before he opened the front passenger door of the zone car. "Get in. I'm taking you to the hospital."

The captain approached the zone car, carrying my shoes, as I climbed into the car and sat down. "Hey, Jason. What's wrong with Danny?"

"Smoke inhalation. Toxic gases." Lieutenant Phelps slammed my door shut. "We need to do a blood gas on him, Ron."

"Sorry about that, Captain," I said, through the open window.

"Shoot, there's nothing to be sorry about." The captain leaned toward the window and handed me my shoes. "Can I do anything for you?"

"Naw. Jason's taking care of me."

"Well." The captain looked at Lieutenant Phelps, who was walking to the driver's side of the vehicle.

"He'll be fine."

"Which hospital are you taking him to?"

Jason got into the zone car and shut his door. "DePaul Hospital."

I released a jagged cough before I pointed to the small heap of turnout gear on the street. "Take care of my gear, Captain."

Concern washed across the captain's face. "Don't worry. I will. You get well."

"I'll be alright."

"Yeah, well—you did a great job. You and Ric should earn a medal for this one."

"Let Ric and Sam know I'm alright." I released another ragged cough as Jason started the engine and shifted into gear.

"I will." The captain backed away from the vehicle.

I let myself relax into the comfort of the zone car's front seat and closed my eyes as Lieutenant Phelps drove me to the hospital—a familiar place for most veteran fire fighters, who usually had a string of in-line-of-duty injuries to their credits.

20

THEY'RE NOT ALIENS

"Dana. Dana. Are you asleep again?"

I opened my eyes. "Yes. And I'm at DePaul Hospital."

Kevin was shocked. "We are?"

"Right back where I started."

"You're not making any sense, Dana. Damn. I've got to get you out of this joint before you crack up. You know, I was in solitary confinement for a hundred and sixty days when I was a POW."

I sat up and swung my feet over the side of my bed. "Was this in Vietnam?"

Kevin scrutinized me with a perplexed expression deforming his face. "What the hell do you think? I'm too young for the First World War."

"Right." I tucked my portable heart monitor into the waistband of my boxer shorts, stood up, maneuvered around my bed table, and walked past the foot of Kevin's bed to get to the window.

Stretched below a grey sky was a landscape of roof tops, which comprised the various levels of the DePaul Hospital's complex. On one of the nearby lower roofs, there were three hard-hatted men working on a large air conditioning unit. As I studied this maintenance crew, Kevin quietly approached the window and stood beside me for a long while.

Kevin pressed his forehead against the window and whispered, "These guys on the roof are real guys. They're not aliens."

I suppressed my amusement. "Yeah. They're real. But are we?"

Kevin turned away from the window and carefully surveyed me. "You're crazy, man."

I kept studying the maintenance workers. "Looks like they're repairing an air conditioner."

Kevin directed his attention back to the crew. "Yeah. Look at all the tools and stuff they have. Can you believe science? Science used to be a firecracker."

"I suppose we've come a long way."

"No supposing about it. We were beating each other with rocks the other day."

I snickered. "You're right."

Kevin sighed.

"What?"

"A beer would taste mighty good right now."

"Just about anything would taste pretty good to me."

"Yeah? Drinking Canadian Mist is not the best or the worst liquor."

With resolve, I continued leaping into whatever direction Kevin was going. "Ah ha."

"But it ain't like drinking zinc," he said.

"Yeah?"

"Yeah. Too much zinc will eat a hole in your stomach and kill you. Even a fifth—no—a pint will kill you. It makes you feel like shit. Once there's a hole in your stomach and the zinc starts leaking through, it's done. It's over. Forget it. You're finished."

"I can believe that."

Kevin sighed and pressed his forehead against the window again in what appeared to be an effort to study the maintenance crew more intensely. "What happened?" he whispered. "I haven't sinned. I raised my kids, worked, went to church. What's up? What did I do? God: I've been straight up and down with you." He twisted his attention toward me, keeping the top side of his head pressed against the window. "But he hasn't told me nothin'." He licked his dry lips. "You know, I'd really like to get out of here."

I pressed my forehead against the closed window and let my gaze travel across the various flat rooftops of the hospital building's complex until my sight lost its focus on a random point along an irregular horizon defined by a brick and mortar architecture.

I wanted to get out of here, too. I wanted to go back to my world, the world that I understood. I knew this heart attack was going to—no, wait. I already knew. This heart attack had fundamentally changed my life. I was afraid my cowboy days were over.

I could not look at Kevin. I couldn't look at myself. A heavy slant of rain burst from the sky and drove the workmen away. This dramatic change caught Kevin's attention.

The heavy downpour reduced the landscape's visibility and contracted my unfocused gaze inwardly. But I could not separate the I from my self.

21

LADDER TRUCK

I was filling-in at Station Ten, which was a three-piece station: an engine, a ladder truck, and the third district battalion chief's car. I was assigned to the ladder truck for twenty-four hours.

Since I was permanently assigned to an engine company, engine work was instinctual while ladder work required thought. Therefore, I was forced to sharpen my ladder skills.

There were five men assigned to the ladder: a driver, a tiller-man, a lieutenant, and two fire fighters on the side. However, the latest departmental rumor indicated that ladder companies were being reduced to four men.

The threat of manpower reduction was a constant, even though there was a lot of rhetoric about fireground safety. Fewer men in the companies always increased the fireground workload and, therefore, increased the rate of injury. This predicament was not the fire department's fault. The city always managed to implement budgetary cutbacks, which affected operational public safety departments, as well as service departments, instead of reducing the army of general administrative personnel.

I stood in front of the ladder truck and leaned toward the closed apparatus door to peer through the door's window at Virginia Beach Boulevard. The street was flooded by the northeaster that was pounding this region of the country. The fifty-mile-an-hour winds forced the heavy rain to fall at an extreme angle. Sudden gusts rattled the door.

"Half the companies are already on the streets," Lenny said, as he approached the apparatus door and stood beside me. "Berkeley's got a working fire."

"It won't be long," I said.

"You feel it, too?"

"We're due for a real bloomer."

"I believe you're right." He took a sip of his black coffee and studied the progress of the storm through the window.

Lenny was Ladder Ten's driver-operator. He was a brilliant fire fighter, and a genuine adept in all the skills of his profession. He was a family man who was rarely home because he always managed to piece together enough hirebacks and cash tricks, in addition to his regular shift, to average twenty full tricks a month in order to support his wife and three daughters.

Lenny was also the kind of fire fighter who was always involved with a project: ladder repair, tool repair, station cleaning, painting, studying the district, training a rookie, and simply taking an honest interest in departmental affairs. Many fire fighters considered him a bit goofy because of his extreme dedication, but he was respected and liked and trusted to be his own man. He was also a guy you wanted at your side when things got tight because there was nobody more aggressive or dependable or knowledgeable on the fireground.

The brass hit, then the watchroom's monitor/radio toned-out all over the station via a network of speakers. "Ten-one house fire. 2901 Tarrant Street. Engine Ten, Ladder Ten, Battalion Three respond to a ten-one house fire at 2901 Tarrant Street. Flames and smoke visible. Time out: 1533."

"That's off of Cape Henry Avenue," Lenny remarked, as he pressed the button that engaged the apparatus door-opener.

Men filtered onto the apparatus floor from all directions: through the watchroom and the galley doors, from the barracks bedroom doors, and by the hallway door leading to the admin offices and the officer bedrooms; one man came from the outside phone cubbyhole and another man came from the workshop at the rear of the station.

What had been a static space filled with parked vehicles had become a beehive filled with activity.

Men dashed to their stations, stepped into their boots, struggled into their turnout coats, and climbed onboard the engine or the ladder or the chief's car without uttering a word; this momentary silence was interrupted by the start-up of diesel engines. Engine Ten had to rev its diesel for several seconds in order to raise the psi gauge reading on its air brakes to the proper limits.

Running lights flooded the apparatus floor, wind and rain swirled through the opened overhead door, radio chatter filled the air, SCBA tank bells rang as men opened their cylinder valves, and three diesel engines roared as they crept smartly onto the apron into the heavy weather. The ladder was on the left side of the station and the engine was on the right side with the chief's car behind it.

Lightning and thunder accompanied the sudden blare of sirens and the increased roar of diesels accelerating onto Virginia Beach Boulevard, where the engine—followed by the chief's car, followed by the ladder truck—took an immediate right onto Azalea Garden Road and raced toward Princess Anne Road at a powerful speed. The streets were flooded. There was little traffic.

As soon as I slipped on my gloves and tightened my helmet's chin-strap, I settled into my wet, open jump seat and contemplated Earth's ancient elements that I was about to be fully immersed in: water, wind, and fire. I loved it. God help me, I loved it.

I smelled smoke as soon as we drove onto Tarrant Street. When I turned around, I saw a three-story brick structure with flames leaping out of two of its third-floor windows. It was a single family dwelling and I hoped everybody was safely out of the house.

Ladder Ten maneuvered around Engine Ten, which had to stop to hook up to a hydrant. Then Ladder Ten drove past Engine Fourteen, which was already on the scene and in command, and stopped near the three-story structure in front of Fourteen.

Five-inch line payed-out of the rear of Ten's hosebed as the piece lumbered to its destination in order to facilitate the line hookup from the hydrant to the five-inch intake adaptor beneath Fourteen's pump panel. As soon as Ten came to a stop, the fire fighter on the side jumped out and hustled to the rear of the engine where he grabbed the five-inch and started pulling out the remaining section. The driver applied the parking brakes, jumped out of the cab, and hurried to the tailboard by the time the five-inch coupling hit the ground. Ten's driver rushed to the right rear compartment, opened its door, and grabbed a set of five-inch spanner wrenches to break the line, while Fourteen's driver attached the five-inch intake adaptor to the engine's main butterfly valve.

As soon as the five-inch line was broken, the driver and fire fighter dragged the line to Fourteen's main intake at the pump panel. The awaiting operator hooked the end of the line to the other end of the five-inch intake adaptor, then radioed the fire fighter at the hydrant to give him water.

Air hissed out of the intake adaptor's bleeder valve as the water filled the line. Then the operator opened the five-inch flow control valve, closed the bleeder valve, then adjusted the pump panel valves until he was satisfied with his gauge readings.

During Engine Company Fourteen's interior fire attack and Engine Ten's hydrant hookup with Fourteen, Ladder Ten hustled to ventilate the roof. Lenny, the driver-operator, engaged the hundred-foot aerial ladder's hydraulic pump after setting the brakes, then jumped out of the cab to chock the wheels. The lieutenant

"Good."

Water cascaded over the steeply pitched roof, making it difficult to maintain traction with my rubber fire boots and forcing me to crawl to the area that needed to be cut open for ventilation.

I located the rafters by sounding with my axe, then I scratched a crude line on the roof's surface with my pick-head to form a rough rectangular outline. Beasely stepped off the roof ladder and perched himself on the roof's ridge above me to make room for Gillis, who set the K-12 on the roof before sitting on the ladder.

Gillis peered at me. "Sure could use a cigarette." Lightning split the sky. "Hell of a way to make a living, ain't it?"

"You love it," I said, as I sat on the roof.

"Shoot. Don't let that damn lieutenant hear you say that." He pulled on the saw's lanyard to get it started. It stalled.

The lieutenant remained on the top of the aerial, while Gillis struggled with the K-12 on the roof ladder.

A crack of lightning split the sky and threatened to kill the world.

"Don't let that K-12 beat you!" the lieutenant hollered.

Gillis grumbled. Beasely watched. I waited.

Gillis kept pulling the lanyard and kept adjusting the choke until it was clear that the K-12 wasn't going to start. He was exhausted. "Won't start!"

"Damn!" the lieutenant shouted.

Beasely eased off the roof's ridge and joined Gillis on the roof ladder. "Give it here."

He handed Beasely the K-12. "It's flooded." Then Gillis climbed up the roof and perched himself on its ridge for a rest.

Beasely fought with the machine until he was exhausted. The saw's motor sputtered and smoked heavily for a few seconds on his last pull, then it died. "Damn." He glanced at the lieutenant. "No way, Lewie."

The lieutenant looked at me. "Start choppin'."

I rolled onto my left knee, anchored my right foot behind me, and began chopping on the downwind side of the planned vent opening.

The *Essentials of Fire Fighting* manual says to rip off the shingles before making the cut. But nobody does that. The book also says to stand on the roof ladder for support. But nobody chops a hole in a roof while confined to a ladder.

I used short strokes; smoke seeped through the cut.

I shifted to the other side of the cut toward the roof ladder to get upwind, crawled toward the roof's ridge, and positioned myself on my knee to make the top cut. I chopped halfway across before repositioning myself.

"Take a break," Beasely said, after he nestled the K-12 on the roof ladder. He eased off the ladder with a pick-head axe.

I didn't argue. I was breathing hard. I eased onto the roof ladder and climbed toward the ridge to sit and watch Beasely finish the top cut.

Before Beasely slid down the roof to make the bottom cut, Gillis snatched the axe out of my hand. "Hold it, Bease. I'll make the bottom cut."

Beasely nodded approvingly and crawled to the roof's ridge to catch his breath.

Gillis climbed down the roof ladder and was able to position himself with one foot on the ladder to make his cut. Smoke poured out of the previous cuts, but the wind carried it away from us. Gillis shifted his position and chopped halfway through the final cut before he gave out and handed the axe back to me.

I waited until Gillis sat on the roof ladder before I positioned myself to make the final cut. I chopped and cursed in an effort to ignore the wind and the rain and the threatening bolts across the sky. Then I used the pick of the axe to begin prying the sheathing boards from the rafters at the bottom of the vent cut. Beasely slid down the roof from the ridge with a halligan tool and pried the boards from the top to help me finish the job.

Black smoke billowed from the large square opening. As soon as Beasely and I shifted further upwind of the large rectangular ventilation hole, Gillis leaned toward the opening with a pike pole and lowered its blunt end through the hole to punch an opening through the ceiling below.

The density of the black smoke increased, as well as the intensity of the heat that accompanied the toxic gases.

The lieutenant keyed his radio. "Ladder Ten, Engine Fourteen."

"Fourteen, . . . ahead."

"Roof ventilated. Roof ventilated."

" . . . four."

Beasely glanced at me. "That ought to help the boys inside."

"Yeah."

And that was the importance of a ladder company's job: to release some of the intense heat and smoke from the interior of the house to allow the attacking fire fighters to reach the seat of the fire and knock it down.

Eventually, white smoke replaced the black. Shortly thereafter, Fourteen's captain announced over the air, "Fire under control. Fire under control."

Behind another bolt of lightning, our lieutenant delivered his brightest command. "Let's get off this damn roof before one of us gets killed."

22

A GENTLE NUT

I OPENED MY EYES from a short, but intense, nap and discovered that my wife of many years was standing at my bedside. Her loving expression warmed my soul and made me smile.

"I'm sorry I took so long to get here," she said.

"Hello, sweetheart. I'm glad you didn't rush. I'm not going anywhere."

Kathleen took hold of my right hand, then leaned over the bed and kissed me. "I brought your poetry book and stuff."

She had draped a shirt with a pair of pants on a hanger across the foot of the bed alongside a toilet bag and book.

"Thanks."

"How are you feeling?"

"Odd. Confused. Weak." Kevin had the television on with the volume turned down. He was watching an auto race. "Looks like my cowboy days might be over."

She sighed. "I'll confess. I won't miss this job of yours."

"I know, I know."

"In fact," she shook her head to display her utter relief, "I'm glad it's over."

"Don't be too grateful. It's who I am."

"You're a lot of other things, too. It's time to change. You're fifty years old and fire fighting is a young man's job. You've said so yourself."

I smiled. "Nag, nag, nag."

"I've never said anything before now. Not after all these years."

"And I appreciate that." I squeezed her hand gently. "I love you."

"I love you, too."

Kathleen's intense but beautiful green eyes registered true concern for me. "Are you in any pain?"

"I get chest pains from time to time. And if the feeling of helplessness can be used as a measure for pain, well . . . you get the idea."

Kathleen squeezed my hand to convey her sympathy. The intimacy of our thirty years of marriage transcended this strange and public place.

I did not want to increase her anxiety, but I had to reveal a bit of my concern. "It's as if a switch inside of me was turned off. My power, it's . . . it's been reduced and . . . and I'm afraid I'll never be the same."

"You're alive and you're going to be alright. That's the important thing."

"Yeah. Right." I wanted to change the subject.

"Wow!" Kevin yelped. "Good pass on the back turn!"

I gazed at the television screen, then turned to Kathleen to convey my bewilderment.

"Is your roommate alright?" she whispered.

I pressed my left forefinger against my lips to amplify our secretiveness. "He's a nut. A gentle nut."

"What's wrong with him?"

"I don't know," I whispered. "But he's delusional."

She grimaced. "Then what's he doing in here with you?"

"I don't know. He calls me Dana."

She giggled. "He seems considerate of our privacy."

"I'll introduce you."

"No, no."

"Kevin? Kevin."

She frowned at me.

"Yeah, Dana."

"This is my wife, Kathleen."

She playfully slapped my arm. "Hello, Kevin."

Kevin sat up on his bed and pulled back the privacy curtain between our beds. He was wearing a pair of glasses with one lens missing and a red ball cap with the logo "Second Enterprise Acceptance Company" printed in front of the hat. "Hello, Kathleen. Nice to meet you. Dana's told me a lot about you."

"I have?"

Kevin laughed. "Dana, me boy, you're a real character."

Kathleen shot an inquiring glance at me. I responded with a shrug.

Kevin suddenly glowered with pain, then began to rub his legs.

"Are you alright?" Kathleen asked.

"My legs. Sometimes the pain is excruciating."

She winked at me. "Is . . . is that why you're here?"

Kevin scrutinized her as if she had told a very bad joke. "What do you think?" He pointed at the television. "I'm a professional race car driver. And that last wreck I had on the track ruined my legs."

"My goodness, I'm sorry."

"Thanks. I appreciate that." Kevin glanced at the television. "Didn't you see the replays?"

"Noo. No, I didn't."

"Ahh. Well. I'll be alright. I'm tough. Like Dana."

"I see," Kathleen said.

"Yeah, they took their sweet time getting me out of that wreck. I really wanted to tongue twist that paramedic's brain. But I knew that would be stupid timing. Especially since my race car was beginning to smoke and burn."

"At least they got you out," I said.

"Oh, yeah. And not a minute too soon."

"Was your wife there?" Kathleen probed.

"Yeah, just before we were separated. She couldn't take the life."

"I understand."

Kevin frowned. "She took the kids."

"I'm sorry."

"Bryon and Shannon. My boy Bryon is ten. Shannon is sixteen and beautiful." Kevin sulked, then he sighed. "Yeah. My wife couldn't take the injuries anymore. Hell, I've broken almost every bone in my body and I'm only twenty-four years old."

Kathleen glanced at me to convey her dismay.

"You're a rough-looking twenty-four," I said jovially, in order to emphasize my ridiculous predicament to her.

"You should've seen my father at twenty-four," Kevin said. "He snored so loud in his sleep that there would be a log cabin outside when I woke up."

"My goodness," said Kathleen.

"You haven't seen my wallet, have you?"

"No," said Kathleen. "I haven't."

Kevin stood up and went to his bedside table. He opened the top drawer and started rummaging through the articles inside. "Where's my wallet? Without it, I can't pay for this room." He counted the gauze pads in the drawer.

"What's he doing now?" Kathleen whispered.

"I don't know," I mumbled. "He's constantly searching through those drawers and counting the things he finds inside them. I don't know why." I indicated the laundry bag. "I can't tell you how many times he's stuck his head in that bag looking for his stolen socks."

"He's funny," she murmured. "At least he's got a sense of humor."

"It's not so funny at three o'clock in the morning."

"I'm sorry, honey. Would you like for me to talk to the nurse and see if you can get another room?"

"I've already tried that, honey. The hospital's full. There's nowhere for me to go. I'm stuck with this crazy man."

Kathleen was crestfallen. She was truly concerned for me.

"I'll be alright. He's harmless. And, well, in my own twisted way, I've grown to like him."

"Can I get you anything?"

"No. You've brought me everything I need."

While Kevin lost himself in his paranoid activity, Kathleen hung my clothes in the room's closet as I arranged my toilet bag and poetry book on my bedside table. This small activity exhausted me.

I reclined undramatically, feeling a little depressed. "You don't have to stay here, honey."

"I don't mind. I brought my own book to read."

"There's no point," I mumbled. "Besides, with Kevin here, there's no privacy. And his constant chatter, well—" I pressed the back of my head against my pillow to suppress my anxiety. "Damn. I wish I were home."

"Soon, sweetheart. You'll be home soon."

A technician entered the room and took my vital signs. Then the floor nurse looked in on me. I introduced her to Kathleen.

When lunch was served, I urged Kathleen to go home. After I convinced her that I was alright, she kissed me and told me she loved me before she left.

After lunch, I lay down on my bed and tried to sleep. But Kevin's presence filled the room and the uncertainty of my future crowded my thoughts. I daydreamed and dozed and wondered why I wasn't restless. Then I remembered that I was in a hospital for a reason. I remembered I'd been short circuited from my restlessness.

The telephone rang: Kathleen was home.

I reminded her not to worry and encouraged her to work on her book. I told her that knowing she was writing her book made me happy—and it did.

I hung up the telephone, after we exchanged kisses, and closed my eyes. I managed to drift, despite Kevin's constant activity.

23

ACTING CAPTAIN

EVERYBODY AT STATION FIFTEEN had the night off except for me and Sam. I was the acting captain and he was the driver and there were two fill-ins on the side: Milton from Station Sixteen and Washington, a hireback from the C-shift.

The August evening was hot and the front and rear overhead doors were open to allow the stillness of the night's humidity to enter the apparatus floor. The bugs were not as aggravating as the sitcom that Milton and Washington were watching on the television in the overly air-conditioned watchroom.

Sam and I sat on the engine's front bumper and slapped an occasional mosquito as we stared at a full moon and listened to Sam's portable radio periodically transmit an outgoing message aimed at other stations.

"Miss Herring wasn't doing well tonight," I said, "when I brought her dinner."

"She hasn't been feelin' right lately. I'm afraid we're goin' to be called over there some night."

"She's about due for a heart attack."

"Or a stroke," Sam emphasized.

"Yeah. For as old as she is."

"I reckon."

We stared into the darkness and waited for the night to unfold itself.

Miss Herring was an eighty-eight-year-old widow who lost her husband to cancer fifteen years ago. She continued to live alone in the house on the immediate west side of the fire station. Years ago, a cook at the station felt concern for her and began to take her a dinner plate prepared from the leftovers, which were always plentiful. This kindness caught on with the other two shifts and developed into a gentle tradition of feeding Miss Herring dinner every night no matter who was cooking.

In time, she began to reciprocate with cakes and pies and cookies—not because she had to, she always said, but because it came from her heart; the boys at Station Fifteen meant a lot to her.

No longer considered an afterthought, the cooks included her in their budget. Miss Herring's dinner plate was prepared and delivered with greater care. And the presence of her unexpected homemade desserts, when she was well enough to bake, became a part of our station's consciousness. In an environment where privacy does not exist and where nothing is left verbally unmolested, this shared kindness between an elderly lady and an entire fire station was left undiscussed.

The stillness of the night encouraged Sam and me to remain silent and attentive for the fire call we were anticipating. This forced me to mentally review the radio and fireground procedures from a supervisory point of view.

The position of acting captain placed a fire fighter into a different dynamic of responsibility and required command skills that were not refined due to infrequent use. Similarly, the other acting position as driver-operator required navigational knowledge of the streets and vehicle performance skills that could not equal the regular driver's sophistication, who had the advantage of daily exercise.

Acting positions were usually filled by a qualified member of the company in rotation with other experienced members. There was a log book that tracked the acting dates for these positions; the fire fighter with the oldest date was up for the acting job, which paid an extra dollar an hour to an acting officer and an extra twenty cents an hour to an acting driver. Needless to say, this so-called compensating pay neither reflected the increased responsibility nor the accompanying stress of unfamiliarity. But occupational pride prevented this monetary insult from developing into resentment. High risk and low pay were occupational norms that were generally tolerated.

Sam's radio toned-out and dispatched Rescue Thirteen on channel two.

"That's us." Sam snatched the radio from the bumper, switched to channel one, and stood up. "We're first-in."

The brass hit, the station's lights came on, and the dispatcher announced, "Ten-one house fire. Engine Fifteen respond to 8000 Ardmore Road on a ten-one house fire. Time out: 2038."

I hustled to the right side of the cab, pulled out my boots, and dropped them on the floor. Then I kicked off my shoes, stepped into the boots, and pulled my turnout pants up to my waist. As soon as I got my suspenders over my shoulders, I climbed into the cab and unhooked the radio handset from the dash. Sam had started the engine, so I transmitted. "Engine Fifteen, responding."

"Ten-four, Engine Fifteen."

Milton pressed the switch to lower the rear overhead door before he ran to his side of the piece and stepped into his boots and nightpants. Washington dressed up to his turnout coat, hustled to the entrance of the forward overhead door, and waited for the engine to creep onto the station's apron before pressing the button to lower the apparatus door.

As soon as Washington climbed onboard the engine, Sam stepped on the accelerator and took a cautious left onto Fishermans Road. When the vehicle straightened out from the turn, he floored the accelerator and hit the siren.

I squirmed into my turnout coat while seated and buttoned up. Then I aimed the gooseneck light over the map book and quickly leafed through the top pages in the index until I found Ardmore Road: map thirty-seven, grid C-3.

Sam honked the air horn as we approached the red traffic light at the intersection of Chesapeake Boulevard and Fishermans Road. I turned to map thirty-seven, as he took a hard left onto the boulevard, and looked for Ardmore, Ardmore, Ardmore, 8000 Ardmore—"There's a hydrant on the corner of Brentwood and Ardmore. But go to the next street—"

"Which one?"

"Dovercourt Road. Take a right on Dovercourt," I said, as I draped the harness of my facepiece over my neck and put on my helmet.

Selecting the southwestern approach to this corner house provided me with a three-sided view: the back and south side, then the front. Thus, improving my visual size-up and, therefore, enhancing my verbal on-scene report to the dispatcher and all incoming units.

"I see smoke!" Washington hollered. "Are we stopping for a hydrant?"

"No!" I said, as I tightened the chin-strap to my helmet. "We're going in!" I placed the mike close to my mouth and keyed the radio. "Engine Fifteen to Engine Thirteen."

"Engine Thirteen, go ahead."

"Pick up the hydrant on the corner of Brentwood and Ardmore on your way in."

"Ten-four."

Sam took a hard right onto Dovercourt. And before I was able to completely assess the scene, Sam took another hard right in front of the house and stopped the engine. I keyed the radio. "Engine Fifteen's on the scene. We have a fully involved single-story frame structure with flames and smoke visible. Engine Fifteen is in the attack mode with Engine Thirteen bringing in a hydrant. Engine Fifteen is in command."

"Ten-four, Engine Fifteen."

The entire front of the house was engulfed in flames. I didn't see anybody on the streets or on the sidewalks, so I didn't know if there was anybody trapped inside.

I managed to tighten my SCBA's harness shoulder straps before pulling the tank out of its jump seat cradle. When I opened the cab's door and stepped off the piece, the intense radiant heat forced me to lower my helmet's faceshield. I managed to see Milton pull the forward line from the crosslay hosebed. "Milton! Take that line to the left side of the house."

"Right!"

"Washington! Take the other inch-and-three-quarters line to the right side." The radiant heat was so intense I was surprised they were able to approach the house.

After placing the engine in pump gear and dropping the tank, Sam cursed himself for stopping so close to the burning house.

"Forget that, Sam!" I hollered, as I cleared Milton's hosebed and encouraged him to clear Washington's. Then, while Sam opened the valves to charge Milton's and Washington's line, I buckled and tightened my SCBA waist strap. I approached Washington but maintained visual contact with Milton.

As soon as their hoses tightened, they bled their lines and adjusted their nozzle settings to a narrow fog stream, which they directed immediately to the burning house. The results were dramatic. I was startled and relieved to see how quickly the fire responded to the water. The house darkened just before Engine Thirteen arrived on the scene with its five-inch hydrant hookup and well before the arrival of Ladder Thirteen, Engine Fourteen, Squad Two, Rescue Thirteen, and Battalion Two.

We were lucky. The house was vacant and we still had paint on the side of Engine Fifteen.

24

KORSAKOFF'S SYNDROME

I HEARD LAUGHTER. Its unfamiliar tone wrenched me from my afternoon slumber.

When I opened my eyes, I saw a doctor and our floor nurse. They were having a conversation with Kevin, who was doing most of the talking.

The doctor laughed openly. "Fascinating. Classic. Simply classic." The remark was clearly addressed to himself.

I shifted onto my left side to study the doctor more carefully.

He was a middle-aged, fair-complexioned, partially bald, clean-shaven, delicately built man with soft hands. He wore a long, unbuttoned white coat over a dress shirt, a tie, and a pair of slacks that were the lower half of an expensive suit.

The doctor squinted at his patient through a pair of round eyeglasses. "So, Kevin, what else have you got to share with me?"

Kevin tilted his head to the left. "Well, Doc, it's a good thing you were standing at the fifty-yard line. Otherwise, I'd have never walked again."

The doctor shot a quick, mischievous glance at the stolid nurse. "You mean, after you caught that long pass?"

"Yeow! I didn't see either of those guys coming. Bam! One tackled me low in front and the other got me high from behind. I was pretzel dough."

"Didn't you get a huge offer from—"

"Yeah! From the Dallas Cowboys! Big news. Big news!" Kevin frowned. Then he rubbed his legs. "Looks like my football career is all over, Doc."

"I'm afraid so, Kevin." The doctor laughed. "Amazing." Without addressing the nurse, he walked out of the room, shaking his head and muttering to himself.

Kevin was unaffected by the doctor's incongruous behavior. He pulled his ball cap lower on his forehead, crossed his arms over his chest, and leaned back against his raised bed. "I think he's suffering from low blood sugar."

The nurse sighed. "Kevin, Kevin. What are we going to do with you?" Kevin did not respond. "You behave."

Kevin's eyes widened. "I haven't done anything. Ask Dana over there."

The nurse gazed at me with sympathy. She had an authoritative smile and a confident stance. She was amazingly attractive despite her uniform white pants, blouse, and sneakers.

"It's alright," I said. "I've become Dana."

She turned to Kevin. "You're not bothering this poor gentleman, are you?"

"No," I said, in Kevin's defense. "He's . . . well . . . I've grown used to him." Kevin remained silent as she directed her attention back to me. "That doctor. Who is he?"

"Dr. Gustufson. Kevin's psychiatrist."

"Ahh. Meaning?"

She approached my bedside and lowered her voice. "Kevin is suffering from what is medically called Korsakoff's Syndrome."

"What in the world is that?" I whispered.

She glanced at Kevin, who was preoccupied with counting the blue, soft-covered Gideon bibles he had collected during his hospital stay. "Since you've been forced to deal so closely with him—"

"That's an understatement."

She bit her lip. "I don't see any harm in telling you."

"I'll be discreet, I promise."

She leaned closer to me. "It's a rarer disease that occurs with chronic alcoholism, which depletes certain B-vitamins and eventually destRics brain cells. The result is permanent and incapacitating memory loss of a specific type."

"But he seems to be capable of some kind of memory," I said.

"That's true. But he's not capable of adding new memory."

"What do you mean?"

"Take yourself, for instance."

"Yeah?"

"You're Dana, right?"

I rolled my eyes for emphasis. "I'm Dana."

"I'll bet you've insisted on your real name many times."

"I've quit calling myself Danny. It's hopeless."

"That's because seconds after you've told him your real name, he forgets it, then hides his memory loss with a made-up name. Medically, or psychiatrically, this is called confabulation."

"God. Is that why he's able to come up with all these stories?"

"Yes."

"And that's his memory loss of a specific type."

"That's right," she said.

"But I'm not sure what you mean when you say he has no ability to set down new memory."

"For immediate events."

"Ahh. You mean, since he can't remember my real name, he covers up this inability by inventing one."

"Exactly. Dana."

"Right."

She grinned. "Your new name is a confabulation."

"And so is everything else he says."

"That's right."

"And that's why, no matter what I say or suggest, he'll be able to seize the information and expand it into a convincing story."

"Incredible, isn't it?"

I glanced at Kevin. "You've got that right."

She nodded. "It's tragic."

"Is there any cure?"

"The doctor says he could be like this for thirty years. Nobody knows."

"Then he's trapped in the made-up details of his consciousness that can't accept new memory. Wow."

"And all because of alcohol," she said.

"I see."

"Be kind to him if you can."

"He's actually a very likeable fellow."

"I know. And how about you? Are you feeling alright?"

"No. But I'm trying to deal with it."

"You need anything?"

"No."

She turned to Kevin. "You behave yourself."

Kevin looked at her like a reprimanded child and remained that way until she left. "God. What a storm trooper she is." Kevin hopped out of his bed, ran to the door, and cautiously peered down the hallway after her.

I rolled onto my back and sighed. "Kevin. Kevin. Go back to bed."

Kevin climbed back into his bed. "You've gotten us into a real pickle this time, Dana."

"I'm sorry."

"Well, what are you going to do about it?"

"I don't know, Kevin. Let's talk about it over dinner."

He looked at his watch. "Did I miss something? That won't be until tomorrow."

"This is tomorrow, Kevin."

His eyes widened. "Jesus. That means I'm getting meatloaf again." Kevin pressed his back against his overly raised bed to express his complete exasperation.

I found myself openly amused, like the doctor. However, I wasn't able to leave. I was trapped in Kevin's upside-down universe that had no room for linear time or present memory. Kevin remained quiet.

I pulled my sheet and blanket up to my chin. I was cold. The air conditioning was set too low.

I closed my eyes and drifted away from the present, as I shivered.

25

WRAPPING THE HYDRANT

A GUST OF FRIGID wind rattled the closed overhead door as I stepped onto the apparatus floor from the watchroom. I approached the metal door, leaned against it, and peered through the window to study the cold street: the night was white and barren and forbidding, and the wind forced the snow to fall at a severe slant.

Another wintry squall pushed a cold draft through the horizontal crack, where the overhead door met the apparatus floor. I shivered, turned away from the door, and approached my side of the piece. Our regular engine was at the Master Mechanic's Shop and we were stuck with one of the old fill-in pieces that had open jump seats.

I inspected my vinyl comfort-bag to make sure I had a dry t-shirt and sweatshirt, a pair of socks and an extra set of work gloves, a woolen watch cap and a towel. After years on the fireground, I'd learned to bring these extra items with me in case I got stuck in the streets all night in bad weather; the bull labor of fire fighting made me sweat to the bone underneath my turnout gear.

There was nothing I could do about the wet condition of my outer turnout gear. But once the heavy work was over and the cold set in, I was able to dry my hair with my towel, change my wet t-shirt, and replace my ice-cold gloves with a dry set. These small comforts made the cold bearable, especially in the wake of a lengthy arson investigation or a demanding overhaul or an all-night fire watch.

The brass hit and the station lights flooded the apparatus floor. "Ten-one house fire. Engine Fifteen respond to 7922 Shore Drive at the El Dorado Trailer Park. Report of heavy smoke showing. Time out: 2014."

The captain keyed his radio as he stepped onto the apparatus floor from his office. "Engine Fifteen, responding."

I hit the switch to open the apparatus door and ran to the right side of the engine. An icy wind blew ferociously into the station as I struggled into my turnout gear.

By the time Ric and the captain climbed onboard, Sam had the engine started, the emergency running lights turned on, and the air breaks released. I hustled to the overhead door and pressed the switch to start the apparatus door closing as soon as the engine crawled out onto the snow-covered apron, then ran to my side of the piece and climbed into my jump seat. Ric smacked the rear window of the cab twice with the flat of his hand to signal Sam that he and I were safely onboard while I reached for my portable radio, which sat in a floor cradle, to turn it on, raise the volume, and set the dial on channel two.

Sam made a careful right onto Fishermans Road, turned on the siren, and steadily accelerated along the treacherously slick road toward Bay View Boulevard, where he made a right.

As soon as I had my turnout coat buttoned, I grabbed my Nomex hood from around my neck and raised it to protect my head and ears from the biting cold. Then I reached around and turned on my SCBA tank before I slipped my arms into its harness straps.

Sam made a hard left on Cape View Avenue. At that new direction of travel, the snow and wind blew into the jump seat. The diesel roared from the engine housing that separated me from Ric, and the siren blared loudly from the roof above.

I buckled my SCBA waist strap, tightened both shoulder straps, then draped my mask harness over my neck. I turned around and saw that we were approaching the East Ocean View Avenue intersection. I braced myself for the turn.

Sam made a hard right and pressed the accelerator to the floor. East Ocean View Avenue was a long, straight shot to where it changed into Shore Drive and ultimately brought us to our destination. The snow and the wind was hitting the engine perpendicularly.

I brought my SCBA facemask to my ear and cracked open my regulator valve, momentarily, to test the air flow. Then I hooked my smoke cutter to the ring on my left shoulder strap, grabbed my portable radio from its floor cradle, and shoved it into my left turnout coat pocket.

I turned around to assess my surroundings. The streets were empty and the engine was flying on an open road covered by a white carpet.

I put on my helmet, tightened the chin-strap, then slipped on my gloves. I looked at Ric. He was ready to go.

"Smoke showing!" he hollered.

I nodded. "One of us will be dropping off!"

Ric's mindful acknowledgement revealed a veteran's understanding.

We relaxed. We listened. We waited for our first command.

The captain slid open the cab's rear window behind me. "Danny!"

I turned around. "Yeah, Captain!"

"Wrap the hydrant on the way in. It's on your side!"

"Right! Got it!"

Ric and I glanced at each other: we knew this was going to be a long, hard night.

The radio chattered. The air horn blared. Other sirens howled in the distance. Sam downshifted. We were approaching the hydrant.

I pulled my tank out of the jump seat's cradle and turned forward to spot the hydrant. As soon as the engine stopped, I stepped off the sideboard and hustled to the rear of the piece. I climbed on the tailboard, unhooked the rope strap attached to the five-inch hydrant adaptor from the handrail, then pulled the adaptor that had a hydrant wrench nestled inside of it from the hosebed. I stepped off the tailboard with the five-inch hose trailing from the adaptor, wrapped the hydrant with the five-inch, dropped the adaptor, stepped on the overlapping hose at the base of the hydrant, and shouted, "Go!" to the captain, who acknowledged me through his opened window and then withdrew into the cab.

As the engine slowly accelerated to pay-out the five-inch line, I took off my helmet and tossed it to the ground, then I unhooked my facepiece harness from my neck and hooked it over my shoulder so the facemask would hang behind me, out of the way.

As soon as the engine traveled far enough away that there was no threat of losing the line, I lifted my foot from the overlapping hose and unwrapped the hydrant. Then I untied the rope strap from the adaptor and freed the hydrant wrench.

I tossed the rope strap aside, clamped the wrench onto the five-inch hydrant cap, and cracked it open. Then I hooked and tightened the wrench to the hydrant stem before I hand-turned the five-inch cap until it dropped open. I checked the arrow's direction near the top stem and turned the wrench in the arrow's direction to flush the hydrant. Black water flowed and quickly became clear through the round opening.

I shut down the water, stooped over to align the adaptor to the hydrant's five-inch male threads, and secured the adaptor into place. Then I stood up, grabbed the hydrant wrench in one hand, lifted the radio to my ear with the other hand, and waited for Engine Sixteen's request for water on the radio or for a long blast from Engine Sixteen's air horn. I got both.

I turned the wrench steadily until the hydrant valve was fully opened and watched the five-inch line fill toward the engine. Then I unhooked the wrench, draped my mask harness around my neck, and donned my helmet.

The snow stopped falling, but the wind grew fiercer. I leaned into the bitter weather and plodded on the slippery road, seeking my engine company.

26

MEATLOAF

"Meatloaf. Meeeeat loaf. Yum." Kevin studied his plate as soon as the food service attendant lifted the thick plastic cover from his tray. "Look at this." He frowned as she turned away from him to set the lid on a straight-backed chair. "It's crap."

The attendant ignored him, left the room, and returned with my dinner tray.

"I hope you've done better than me," said Kevin, as soon as the lady lifted my thick plastic tray cover.

I winked at the grinning attendant. "I got roast beef and mashed potatoes, Kevin. Do you want to trade?"

"I wouldn't do that to my worse enemy."

The food service attendant chuckled warmheartedly. "Behave yourself, Mr. Brooke, and eat your dinner."

"Behave myself, she says." He examined his food, then feigned delight. "Yum." Then he impaled the meatloaf with the fork and left it standing perpendicularly to his plate.

The attendant left the room.

I pretended to ignore him and started eating my food.

Kevin leaned toward the fork until his mouth was a couple of inches away from the handle and began speaking as if it were a microphone. "And that's a high fly ball out to center field a-n-d, he's out of there at the bottom of the eighth inning, folks."

"Eat your food, Kevin."

Startled by my remark, Kevin looked at his plate. "Oh. Is that what this is?" He rolled his tray table toward my side and swung his legs over the edge of the bed. "Eating alone is a drag. Come on. Join me."

I pushed my tray table toward his side and sat up on the edge of my bed. "Sure."

Kevin vigorously shook a can of strawberry Boost, opened it, and drank it to the bottom. He held up the can and displayed it next to his face as if he were performing a television commercial. "I like this stuff. It's great! But it's disgusting without lemon in it. Have you got a lemon?"

"I'm fresh out, Kevin."

He placed the empty can on his tray. "It's just as well. Drinking this stuff is a bad habit to get into."

"I guess."

"No guessing about it, Dana. Eat your roasted loaf. Now that's good for you."

We ate our dinner and we shared our desserts and we sank into a quiet period after our trays were taken away. But before I fell asleep, the telephone rang. Kevin answered the phone, but the call was for Dana. He waited for me to lift my phone off the cradle before he hung up.

"Hello? Hi, honey. Ah. Yes. Dana. Ha, ha. Very funny." I cupped the receiver with my hand. "Kathleen says hi." Kevin gave me a thumbs up. I uncovered the receiver. "Kevin says hi back." We exchanged laughter. "I'm doing alright. And you? Did you get any rest? Good. Me? I'm fine. Really. Kevin is looking after me." We exchanged more laughter. "Did you call Mom? Good. Did you tell her not to worry? I know, I know. Good. You gave her this number? Then she'll call. I'm fine, honey. Really. There's no need for you to visit tonight. Stay home and do your work. That will make me very happy. Besides, I've got all the company I can handle." I chuckled. "Right. Kathleen says goodbye, Kevin."

His eyes widened. "Is that really Kathleen?"

"She says, behave yourself."

"Goodbye, Kathleen!" His expression grew serious. "My God, it's been years."

"Did you hear that, honey?" I chuckled. "Yeah. Kevin says it's been years. See what I mean? Stay home." I laughed. "It's insane. I've had a heart attack and it's insane. No, no, no. I didn't mean to worry you." Then I had to explain what I meant and continue to assure her that I was perfectly alright before I was able to hang up the telephone and close my eyes and ignore Kevin rummaging through the laundry bag in search of his green socks.

I drifted. I daydreamed. I heard the distant call of a "signal one." I heard the familiar shrill of a whistle. I heard . . .

27

SIGNAL ONE

"SIGNAL ONE, SIGNAL ONE!" Ric's shrill whistle followed. "Don't let it get cold, boys. Signal one."

I was lying down in the dark barracks bedroom when Ric announced dinner over the station's intercom. I sat up on my bed, feeling tired and not especially hungry. But I forced myself out of bed so Ric wouldn't fret over his prepared meal.

I shuffled across the bedroom and pushed past the double doors leading onto the apparatus floor. The brightness of the late afternoon day assaulted me.

As I stretched, I saw the captain step onto the apparatus floor from his office and hustle toward the galley via the watchroom. Sam was already fixing his plate when I walked into the galley just ahead of the captain.

"I posted this month's union announcements in the watchroom's bulletin board," the captain said, as he entered the galley.

Nobody responded.

"Tea or water, Captain?" said Ric, who was throwing ice into four plastic glasses.

Ron, our captain, studied the array of simmering pots on the stove, then glanced at the huge roast on the kitchen counter that Ric had sliced on the cutting board. "Tea."

"Water for me," I said, as I grabbed two plates from the sink's drainboard and handed one to Ron, who was an old personal friend of mine; a friendship born before either one of us joined the fire department and a friendship that remained strong through the years.

Ron had the reputation for being a private's captain, which meant he never forgot his tailboard roots—the place where we all came from in this profession. He was democratically minded and intelligent and supervised his men fairly. He was also honest, administratively meticulous, and decisive on the fireground.

I stabbed a couple of slices of roast with the serving fork and flopped them on my plate, then I turned to the stove to dress out my plate with mashed potatoes and gravy as well as collard greens and a roll, when I noticed the beginning of Sam's performance. He was staring at the hot tray of brown yeast rolls sitting on the stove's counter above the pots.

"Damn, look at this," he said. "Where are the charcoal brickets?"

"Screw you," said Ric.

The captain giggled as he stabbed a couple of slices of roast with the serving fork and laid the well-done meat on his plate.

I grinned mischievously. "Check the bottom of your roll before you take a bite. You could break a tooth."

Ric pouted. "You all get off my rolls. Just because I burned them last time—"

"And every other time this cycle," Sam added.

"That's not true," I said. "He never got the chance to burn his rolls the last time, remember?"

Sam snapped his fingers. "Oh, yeah, that's right. We got flat hockey pucks instead."

"Eat me," Ric said. "I can't help it if the yeast don't rise."

Ron picked one of the rolls from the pan. "Listen." He tapped it against the side of the stove. "I think we're safe, boys."

Ric chose to ignore the captain and set the glasses of tea and water on the table. Then he grabbed a plate from the drainboard and hustled the captain toward the other side of the stove so he could prepare his own plate. "Are you all goin' to eat or keep messin' with me?"

"Everything looks great, Ric," I said, with animation, in order to encourage the others to shower him with the compliments he deserved.

"Sure."

"Great!"

"Wonderful."

"This is a culinary delight."

By the time Ron and Sam finished pouring on their exaggerated praise, they were seated at the galley table with full plates set before them. Ric was appeased despite their devilish behavior.

The long wooden table with a green Formica top was arranged along the wall that separated the galley from the apparatus floor. A wooden bench, which could accommodate four men, ran the length of the table on both sides. However, since there were only four of us, we sat near the corners of the table: the captain with his back to the wall with me facing him and Sam with his back to the wall with Ric facing him. I sat near the stove, on the watchroom's door side of the galley, and Ric sat near the refrigerator, microwave, and coffee pot, on the apparatus' door side. Behind Ric and me were the kitchen sink, a large window, and a counter that ran the length of the galley. There were cupboards on both sides of the window, which had a large air conditioning unit perched in it, and underneath the counter were an array of lower drawers and cabinets for pots and pans and utensils.

The floor was covered with reddish-brown tile and the walls were painted an institutional green. The galley was strictly a utilitarian space, which struggled against the abuse of constant use.

The galley was also the heart of the fire station in the same way the watchroom was the mind.

I took a bite of my mashed potatoes and almost burned my tongue.

The brass hit. "Fire alarm. Engine Fifteen respond to 7000 Auburn Avenue at the Braywood Manor Apartments on a fire alarm. Time out: 1723."

The captain stood up, grabbed his portable radio from the table, and headed to the apparatus floor through the watchroom. Sam took a quick bite of his roll before he left the galley through the door on his side. Ric shot a disgruntled glance at me before we stood up to leave. "Damn, how do they know?"

"It'll keep," I said, optimistically.

The sound of the diesel starting up encouraged us to hustle out of the galley.

Ric ran to the rear of the station and hit the switch to lower the overhead door as I went to the front of the station. I waited for the engine to pull out onto the station's apron and for Ric to reach me before I pressed the switch and stepped outside with him as the overhead door lowered. Ric opened the right jump seat door and let me climb in before he stepped up into the compartment and slammed the door behind him.

"We're in!" I shouted, as Ric stepped over my boots and squeezed past me to get to his side.

Sam caught us off guard and took a hard left onto Fishermans Road with lights and sirens and speed. Ric tumbled toward me as I was thrown against the closed door and its rolled up window.

"Damn," Ric said.

"You alright?"

"Yeah." He steadied himself and shuffled to his side to get into his gear. "Are you?"

"I'm okay," I said, as I kicked off my shoes and stepped into my boots.

We braced ourselves as soon as the engine reached Chesapeake Boulevard, knowing Sam was going to take another hard left. Ric's helmet and my smoke cutter fell to the ground during the inside of the turn.

"Go, Samuel!" Ric said.

Sam was driving faster than usual for whatever unknown reason. Adrenalin affected each of us differently, depending on the alarm's time of day and the fire fighter's current mental disposition.

Ric and I were dressed up and strapped down by the time we crossed Little Creek Road. We were second-in engine on this call and Engine Fourteen usually made a right turn onto Johnston Road from the opposite direction just before we followed them with a left turn. Then we made an immediate right onto Auburn Avenue and went to the Branch Road intersection to stand by a hydrant while Fourteen Engine proceeded to the main entrance of the high-rise building to disembark and go inside to investigate the cause of the alarm.

Ladder Fourteen, Squad Two, Battalion Two, and Rescue Fourteen also stood by in their designated street positions and waited to be cleared from the routine false alarm. I stared into the distance through my side window.

"That roast is goin' to be tougher than boot leather when we get back," Ric complained.

"Go on," Sam quipped. "Blame it on the fire alarm."

Ric grinned sheepishly, stood up, and leaned over the back of the jump seat toward Sam. "Damn, I'm goin' to nail your plate to the wall if you keep messin' with me."

Sam responded with a giggle, which infected the captain.

"Don't worry, Ric," I said.

He sat down. "I'm not."

"The microwave will bring the meal back."

"Yeah."

I stared into the distance through my window for several more minutes.

"Engine Fourteen, Dispatcher."

"Dispatcher, go ahead."

"Clear all units with the exception of Engine Fourteen."

"Ten-four, Engine Fourteen. Clear all units responding to 7000 Auburn Avenue with the exception of Engine Fourteen."

Sam released the air brakes as the captain switched channels and cleared Engine Fifteen, which meant we were back in commission and available to respond to the next fire call.

I waved at Ladder Fourteen as we drove by the standing vehicle, and Ric waved at Squad Two as it traveled past us in the opposite lane. Then we disengaged ourselves from our SCBA tank harnesses and stripped out of our turnout gear as Sam took us back to our station. By the time we reached Little Creek Road, our tanks were turned off and their high pressure lines bled, our harness straps were readjusted and draped along the back of the jump seats, our turnout coats were peeled off and hung on the bulkhead, and our nightpants were dressed down over our boots and set aside.

I slipped on my shoes as we reached the traffic light on the intersection of Little Creek Road and Chesapeake Boulevard. When the light turned green and allowed Sam to accelerate, I leaned back against my jump seat feeling bored and deprived of an appetite.

As we approached the station, the captain pressed the door opener, which hung from the cab's sun visor, to raise the apparatus door. Sam angled past the front driveway and stopped, waited for Ric and I to open our doors and jump out of the piece to restrain traffic in both directions, then backed the engine into the station while the captain keyed his radio.

"Engine Fifteen's in quarters."

"Ten-four, Engine Fifteen."

Sam killed the engine as Ric and I reached the apparatus floor, then the four of us dispersed. I went into the watchroom to reset the monitor and wash my hands in the small bathroom. The captain went to the office to record the run number and times in the log book and wash his hands. Ric went into the galley to wash his hands and save the meal. And Sam secured the engine before going to the barracks-side bathroom to wash his hands. When we converged upon the dead meal, we avoided teasing Ric in order to prevent a genuine argument.

We heated our dinner plates in the microwave and attacked our meals with forced enthusiasm.

"The chief is coming by tonight with the minutes of this afternoon's meeting," Ron said.

"Anything important?" Ric asked.

"Not that I know of."

I bit into a piece of gristle just as the brass hit.

"Power line down. Engine Fifteen, respond to 1363 Baychester Avenue on a power line down. Time out: 1759."

Ric threw his fork on his plate, stood up, and stormed out of the galley in disgust. Sam quietly followed him out as I shot through the watchroom ahead of Ron.

The captain keyed his portable radio. "Engine Fifteen's responding."

With the emergency running lights already flashing, Sam took a lazy right turn onto Fishermans Road and accelerated the engine to half-speed, knowing this was not a high priority incident. In fact, he did not turn on the siren until we approached Bay View Boulevard.

After a right turn and a quick left, we were on Beaumont Street heading for Baychester, where we would take a left.

Ric and I slipped into our boots, raised and buckled our nightpants to our waists, and maneuvered our suspenders over our shoulders. Then we sat down and waited, knowing there wouldn't be much for us to do after we arrived on the scene.

Once we were on Baychester, Ric and I stood up and looked forward over our jump seats to help Sam and the captain locate the downed power line.

"There it is," said Ric. "On the left. Look, it's also arcing off that tree."

Sam saw the line and stopped the engine across the street to stay clear of it.

The captain keyed his radio. "Engine Fifteen's on the scene."

"Ten-four, Engine Fifteen."

Ric and I donned our helmets, slipped on our gloves, and stepped off the piece to investigate. The end of the power line sparked and sizzled a couple of times as we crossed the street and cautiously approached it.

"There's nothing we can do about this," Ric said.

I pointed at the top of the closest power line pole. "Damn. Look at the arc burning through that fallen tree branch." The captain approached us. "See that, Ron?"

"Yeah."

"Do we have an ETA yet?"

"The dispatcher gave me fifteen minutes."

Ric chuckled. "I'll believe that when I see the Virginia Power truck." He looked at his wristwatch. "Fifteen minutes."

Several residents poked their curious heads through their opened front doors and chose to remain within the safety of their homes. But an elderly woman, accompanied by a girl, decided to venture toward us.

"Danny, keep those two away from here," said Ron.

"Right, Captain." I maneuvered around the live wire and the damaged pole and approached the elderly woman and what appeared to be her granddaughter.

"Good evening, ma'am."

"Is everything alright?" she asked.

"Yes, ma'am. Everything's fine. VEPCO will be here shortly."

"We've no electricity."

"Yes, ma'am."

"It's going to ruin dinner."

"I'm sorry, ma'am. Virginia Power will be here soon to repair the damage."

She squinted at Ric and the captain and the sputtering line. "Is it serious?"

"No, ma'am. But it can be very dangerous if you get too close to that hazard."

"Oh, dear."

"As you can see, that power line is alive."

"Yes. We heard the line pop."

"Ma'am, I'd feel a whole lot better if you'd take this nice young lady back into the house with you where it's safe. There's nothing you can do out here but get hurt."

The section of the power line that was wedged underneath the broken branch on top of the pole arced and sizzled. Then a small blue-yellow flame flared into existence and continued burning from the branch.

"Oh, my!" The elderly lady took hold of her granddaughter's hand.

"Nothing to worry about, ma'am. Please, go inside."

After I saw them go back into their house, I approached the rear of the idling engine. "What's up, boys?"

"Not much," said Ron.

I sat on the tailboard next to Ric. "Looks like we're having another fine fire department day."

Ric sulked. "My taters are goin' to be harder than concrete by the time we get back."

"A spoonful of gravy and a minute in the microwave will take care of that," I said.

Ric did not want to be convinced.

"Looky here," said Sam.

A VEPCO truck approached us and stopped behind the engine. The lineman leaned out of his rolled-down window and addressed the captain. "What have we got?"

The captain approached him as he pointed at the pole. "Over there. See? It's alive. And up there. It's burning."

The rest of us shuffled toward the side of the engine and climbed onboard. Late afternoon was becoming early evening. Ric and I pulled off our gloves, pushed our nightpants down to our ankles, and kicked off our boots.

"Miss Herring can have my plate when we get back," Sam said, to agitate Ric.

"It doesn't matter," I said, before Ric was able to respond. "She always saves whatever we bring her for the next day," I slipped on my shoes.

Ric decided to ignore Sam but grudgingly acknowledged my statement as he slipped on his shoes.

The captain opened his door and climbed into the cab. "Let's go."

Sam turned off the running lights and released the air brakes, as the captain slammed the door shut and nestled himself comfortably into his jump seat. Then he keyed the radio to clear the scene, as Sam accelerated the engine.

"Engine Fifteen, dispatcher."

"Go ahead, Engine Fifteen."

"Engine Fifteen is in the clear."

"Ten-four, Engine Fifteen, at 1838. Incident number, 13682."

"Thirteen, six-eighty-two. Ten-four."

As soon as I relaxed into my jump seat and mentally zoned out, the dispatcher toned-out another run.

"Engine Fifteen. Report of a stabbing. Respond to 3022 East Ocean View Avenue at the Breakers Motel. Time out: 1839."

Sam hit the lights and siren as the captain keyed the radio.

"Engine Fifteen's responding."

"Ten-four, Engine Fifteen. NPD is en route to the scene."

"Ten-four, dispatcher."

"Thirteen Engine must be out," said Ric.

I shrugged my shoulders. "I guess."

My helmet fell off the empty jump seat next to me and bounced on the floor. I bent over to retrieve it but had to brace myself against the turn Sam was making. I grabbed my helmet as we came out of the turn, replaced it on the jump seat next to me, then leaned back into my seat and settled into the ride.

There were four jump seats facing the rear bulkhead of the enclosed two-door compartment that had enough head room for even the tallest fire fighter to remain standing if he chose to do so. Ric sat on the left window seat, watching the road go by, and I sat on the right, doing the same. Two empty jump seats separated us. There were also two spring-loaded, pull-down seats attached to the opposite bulkhead, which we occasionally sat on during ordinary travel and administrative runs like schools or high-rise inspections. If necessary, six fire fighters could ride comfortably in the jump seat compartment.

Ric handed me a set of non-sterile latex examination gloves from the box. "Here you go."

"Thanks."

We gloved up, expecting to see blood. Both of us disliked medical calls.

The engine reached the East Ocean View straightaway in no time, then flew down the avenue toward the third-rate motel-apartment building occupied by the poorer segment of Ocean View's society—people who were usually a single week's rent away from being homeless.

When we arrived on the scene, Ric shuffled through the door on my side to assist me. I raised the center storage compartment door and grabbed the large, blue resuscitation bag and the black trauma bag. Ric snatched out the red heart monitor and the small, orange medical box. We hustled around the front of the engine as the captain stepped down from the cab of the piece.

I saw several people waving at us. "Over there, Ric."

We lumbered toward them like pack animals.

"What's goin' on?" Ric asked.

One of the ladies pointed down the open-air corridor toward the rear of the motel. "He's sittin' on the other side of those steps."

"Thank you, ma'am," I said, as we continued toward our uncertain destination.

As soon as we got past the rear of the cement stairwell, we discovered a shirtless man sitting calmly at the foot of the steps. He was leaning against a wrought-iron banister and studying the five-inch gash across the right side of his broad, muscular chest; blood seeped from the wound.

"What happened to you?" Ric asked, as we set down our gear.

"She got mad."

"I reckon so." Ric opened the black trauma bag to hunt for the four-by-fours, the roller gauze, and the tape.

I leaned toward the man to study the angry pink slash. "What kind of blade did she slice you with?"

"A steak knife."

"Lord," Ric remarked. "Your wife?"

"Uh-huh."

"Damn." Ric handed me a wad of four-by-fours. "What the hell did you say to her?"

"Nothin'."

"Yeah, well—this is a lot of nothin'." I used the gauze to wipe some of the blood from his chest.

I heard a nearby door burst open on the second floor.

"Oh, Lord," said Ric. "Look out, Danny."

An angry lady appeared at the top of the stairs brandishing a serrated knife with a brown, plastic handle. The stainless steel blade glistened with blood. She looked down at her husband with fiery eyes. "Don't you come back in this house, you hear!?"

Another lady, who was already standing on the second-floor landing, called to her. "Talisha. Talisha! Where are you goin', child?"

Talisha turned away from her husband and stormed back into the apartment, leaving the door open. The lady followed her inside and slammed the door shut.

"Lord, God," said Ric. "Where the hell is NPD?"

"I don't know," I answered, as I saw the captain approach us. "Where's NPD, Cap?"

Ron shrugged his shoulders. "They should be here by now."

I discarded the bloody four-by-fours. "Well, his old lady is still running wild with a knife in her hand."

"She's madder than a hornet," Ric added.

I took the additional four-by-fours that Ric offered me, separated them into two thick bandages, and pressed them against the man's wound. "That hurt?"

"No."

The captain stepped away from us and keyed his portable radio. He gave the dispatcher a situation report followed by a superfluous request for NPD.

"What's your name?" I asked the injured man.

"Franklin Thomas."

"Okay, Franklin. We're going to fix you up here. Let us know if it hurts, alright?"

Franklin nodded. "I oughta bust her face."

Ric suppressed his amusement, then extended sympathy to the man. "Easy there, Franklin. No use gettin' any madder than you are. Women can sure put a hurtin' on you if you don't watch out." He climbed the stairs to get behind the man. "Sit forward a little, Franklin."

The man leaned forward as I maintained pressure against his wound. Ric knelt on the stairs and rolled the gauze dressing over the four-by-fours, then under his right armpit and above his shoulder to secure the bandage in place.

When NPD arrived, the captain escorted the two police officers to us.

"A domestic," I said to one of them. "His wife is in that apartment up there. Her name's Talisha."

"Be careful," the captain added. "She's still got a knife in her possession."

I caught the silent exchange between the police officers, which revealed their discomfort. None of us in public safety—police, fire, or rescue—liked incidences involving domestic violence. These situations were extremely unpredictable and dangerous. At that moment, I was particularly glad to be a fire fighter instead of a cop.

They climbed the stairs to the second-floor landing and approached the motel-apartment. One of the officers stepped aside while the other identified himself. "Police! Open up!"

"Is she alone?" the backup officer asked.

"She's with another lady." I looked at Franklin for assistance.

"A friend," he said. "A next-door neighbor."

"She's with a girlfriend," I projected to the officers. "I think she's trying to console her." I noticed that Franklin appreciated the softer edge I was attempting to convey.

The officer at the door knocked harder. "Police department." He grabbed the doorknob to test the lock. "Open this door!"

Both officers drew their nightsticks from their belts.

The captain glanced at me. "Whoa."

The lead officer stepped back from the threshold after he heard the doorknob rattle. When the door swung open, Talisha's friend presented herself. "She's alright now. She was upset."

"Who are you?" the officer demanded.

"A friend."

"Have your friend come outside."

"She ain't got a knife no more."

"Where is it?"

"On the kitchen table."

The officers looked at each other with apprehension. The one by the door had the lady step back into the room, away from the threshold, so he could peer inside the motel-apartment. He seemed comforted by what he saw, then he entered. His partner followed him inside and shut the door.

Ric let out a long sigh. "Lord. Your old lady must really be pissed off."

Franklin sheepishly lowered his head. "Yeah."

When Rescue Sixteen showed up, Ric and the captain gave one of the paramedics a full medical report in order to properly turn Franklin over to them.

The other paramedic approached me. "Hey, Danny."

"What's up, Jason?"

"Same ol', same ol'." After quickly sizing up the situation, he interrupted Ron. "Thanks, Captain. You all can clear up. We've got him."

"Are you sure?"

"Nothing to it. Mike and I can handle it."

"NPD is in that apartment with his wife," Ron added, as Ric and I packed up our medical equipment.

Jason looked at Franklin and grimaced. "Is she the one—"

"Yep," the captain interjected for Franklin.

"Hmm. Can you walk to the ambulance with us or do you need a stretcher?"

Franklin stood up. "I can walk."

"Good." Jason waved at us. "Thanks, guys."

"Later, Jason." I tapped his partner, Mike, on the shoulder. "Take it easy, Mike."

"I'm tryin'."

"You sure you all don't need any help?" Ric asked.

"Naw, Mike and I have got it."

"Alright," said Ric. "Later."

Sam was waiting for us at the piece. "Anything to it?"

"Nothin' worth talkin' about," Ric said.

"Let's get out of here," said the captain.

"That works for me." I lifted the large resuscitation bag into the compartment and got out of Ric's way in order for him to place the monitor and med box beside it. Then I stuck the small trauma bag on top of the med box.

I walked toward the street as Ric shut the side storage compartment door and waited for Sam to start backing the engine out of the parking lot. As soon as I heard the backing bell, I stepped into the street to stop oncoming traffic. Ric acted as a safety guide by walking ahead of the engine near the left rear side.

I had the traffic stopped by the time the engine reached me. Sam quickly backed into the street until he was facing the right direction, then he stopped the engine and waited for Ric and me to climb onboard and shut our side-doors before driving away from the scene.

"The running lights!" Ric hollered. "They're still on."

Sam switched off the emergency running lights, as he continued accelerating, while the captain cleared us with the dispatcher, putting us back in commission.

There was no traffic on Fishermans Road when we got back to the firehouse, so Ric and I didn't bother getting out of the engine to help Sam back into the station.

The captain keyed the radio. "Engine Fifteen's in quarters."

"Ten-four, Engine Fifteen."

I went to the watchroom to reset the monitor, the captain went to his office to get his run times on the inside line, Sam went to the rear of the station to open the apparatus door, and Ric went into the galley to assess the damage. After completing our small tasks, we converged in the galley.

Dinner had lost all its appeal. There wasn't much to say, so none of us bothered. We simply dumped the cold food on our plates into the trash can and began cleaning the galley.

Ron started clearing the table. Sam poured liquid detergent into the sink after plugging the drain, then started the hot water running to wash dishes.

I grabbed a couple of clean plates from the cabinet and handed one to Ric. I transferred the leftover roast from the cutting board into my plate and Ric fixed Miss Herring her dinner in the other.

"Don't bother savin' anything but the roast," said Ric.

"I saw Bear sniffing around in the back," Sam said, without turning away from the sink.

"So did I."

"Let him have some roast," said Ric.

"Of course," I said. "I plucked the meat scraps from our plates."

"Well—go on and add a few good pieces. There's plenty."

"I planned to."

After clearing the table and placing the butter and condiments back into the refrigerator, Ron got a clean, wet rag to wipe down the table top. By the time I finished dumping the rest of the cold and congealed food into the trash can, Sam had finished the dishes and was ready to scrub the pots that I set on the counter beside him. Ric left the galley carrying Miss Herring's dinner and Bear's plateful of scraps.

Ric was not expected to return to the galley once he completed these errands. It was the cook's well-earned privilege not to help with galley cleanup after meals.

Traditionally, the man doing the dishes, pots, and pans did not have to do anything else in the galley after dinner. That left Ron and me to clean the stove top and counters, wipe down all dirty surfaces and appliances, sweep the floor, dry the dishes, take out the trash, prepare a bucket of soapy water with a mop from the deep sink in the hose room and roll it near the galley door leading into the apparatus floor, start a fresh pot of coffee, dry the pans and replace the pots into their respective cabinets, and clean whatever needed to be cleaned before mopping ourselves out of the galley and dumping the dirty pail of water into the hose room's deep sink. Then we'd wait for the floor to dry before pouring ourselves our evening coffee.

These small rituals and divisions of labor gave station life some order in an occupation faced with constant disorder.

"Fresh pot!" Ric announced, as soon as the galley floor was dry enough to walk on. "Fresh pot!" Ric poured the coffee.

28

PROTOCOL

DESPITE THE CHIEF's enthusiastic delivery, the superficiality of the departmental minutes reduced us to the state of utter boredom. Since our battalion chief was one of the good guys and a friend, we controlled our restlessness and gave her the full attention she deserved. After she left, we discovered there was nothing interesting to watch on the television.

The evening was quiet and the station felt dull, and none of us were in a talkative mood.

We roamed the station like dispirited ghosts. Sam sat on the park bench situated in front of the station and studied the stars. Ric went to the parking lot at the rear of the station and sat on the picnic table under the tree. Ron disappeared into his office to catch up on his fire reports and finish the daily report. And I sat down in the telephone cubby-hole and called my wife.

Kathleen was glad I called. Her work was going well today and she was anxious to confide her intellectual discoveries with me. She was writing a very important book of philosophy that dealt with ethics—specifically, a discourse on the virtue of charity. After thirty years of marriage, we still shared our ideas and respected each others' ideals. She was a brilliant woman and I loved her deeply.

Toward the end of our long conversation, Ric began walking by the telephone booth. He was getting restless about calling home.

I told Kathleen I had to go. She sent me a parting kiss, then told me to be careful before we hung up.

I waved at Ric as I crossed the apparatus floor, then went into the barracks bedroom. I considered going to my locker to get my novel, but I decided I was too tired to read.

I went into the bathroom, washed up, brushed my teeth, and trotted back into the bedroom where I turned off the lights, took off my trousers and shoes, and tried to go to sleep early.

The air conditioner droned white noise and blew cold air across the barrack's darkness. I was still awake when I heard Sam and Ric quietly ease into their racks. I pretended to be asleep.

I was startled when the brass hit. I had fallen asleep.

"Difficulty breathing. Engine Fifteen respond to 1114 Sheppard Avenue on a report of chest pains, difficulty breathing. Time out: 0113."

I got out of bed, grabbed my trousers from the chair next to my bed, and struggled into them before slipping into my shoes. When I glanced back to see if Sam and Ric were up, I discovered they were a few steps behind me.

The forward overhead door was open and the engine was running by the time Ron stepped onto the apparatus floor to join us. When he and Ric climbed onboard, Sam drove the engine onto the apron. I pressed the button to close the apparatus door, dashed out to the piece, slammed the side-door closed after I climbed onboard, and heard Ric holler, "Let's go!"

Sam took a hard left onto Fishermans Road and took another left, shortly thereafter, on Pythian Avenue.

I handed Ric a set of rubber gloves from the box and took a pair out for myself. I stuffed them into my pocket instead of putting them on.

Sam took a right on Sheppard Avenue and, after passing five houses on the right, we were there. Ric followed me out through the door on my side, like he always did on medical calls, and helped me carry the usual medical equipment to the house: I grabbed the blue resuscitation bag and he grabbed the red monitor.

A young woman, dressed in a nightgown and a bathrobe, was waiting for us at the opened front door. "Hurry, please, my husband's inside."

"What's wrong?" I asked, as I approached her.

The terror registered in her eyes reached me before she whispered. "I don't know." She grabbed the front of her robe with her trembling right hand. "I don't know."

Ric handed me the monitor. "Rescue Thirteen's here. I'm going to help them bring in the stretcher and stuff."

"Good. I'll see what's going on. Hurry."

The lady led me into the living room where a partially bald man, who looked to be in his late thirties, was sitting on the floor with his legs extended in front of him. He appeared dazed and he was having difficulty supporting himself in this position even though he was bracing himself upright with both arms.

I encouraged the man to lie down, as I approached him, but he refused. I placed the blue medical bag, that contained the oxygen resuscitator, and the red monitor on the floor beside him. "Has he been drinking?"

"No," she said. "All we had was popcorn and Diet Coke earlier this evening, while we were watching television."

"I see."

"We went to bed hours ago. But Harry woke up feeling bad."

"How long ago?" I knelt down beside Harry, observing his disorientation.

"I . . . I don't know. Fifteen . . . maybe, twenty minutes ago."

"Was he in pain?"

"He said he couldn't breathe. He said his chest felt tight."

"Hello, Harry. I'm here to help you. Tell me what's going on inside of you." The man looked at me with intense curiosity. "Are you having any chest pains right now?" I opened the blue medical bag and started setting up the oxygen for him. I was beginning to wonder what was taking Ric and the boys on the rescue unit so long. "Talk to me, Harry. I'm here to help you."

The man's face lost all expression. His arms went limp. Then he slowly lowered himself to the floor until he was flat on his back.

"Oh my God," his wife murmured. "What's wrong with him? What's happening?"

I quickly placed the nonrebreathing oxygen mask over his mouth and nose and maneuvered the elastic band behind his head to secure it. When I probed him with another question, he suddenly sat up, lifted his legs off the ground, and balanced himself on his coccyx bone. Then his arms tensed and shot upward, as if he were reaching for the sky, and his fingers spread convulsively, as if he were trying to latch onto something. After this explosive tension reached a climax, his head and limbs went limp, his eyes rolled up and back until both pupils disappeared behind his lids, his torso deflated, and he collapsed—his life imploded.

I instantly knew he was a hopeless code. But because of my lowly EMS level of medical training and because of his wife's presence, I refrained from conveying my personal impression when the Rescue Thirteen paramedics finally arrived.

"I think we have a code." I stepped over the patient to get out of McCormac's and Azuela's and Allen's way.

I was surprised to see three guys riding on the rescue unit. "What are you doing on the bucket, Allen?"

"This is my ride-time to finish certifying for cardiac tech."

"I see." I knelt beside Harry again.

As soon as the three medics became preoccupied with the patient, I surreptitiously placed my hand on the unconscious man's forearm to see if I could transfer some of my own life's force into him. But before there was any possibility for my energy to have any effect, the Rescue Thirteen boys crowded me away from the man with their medical bags and monitors and drug boxes, as well as with the intense flurry of medical assessments and monitor hook-ups preceding CPR, as well as an intravenous startup and drug prep. Then Ric aggressively pushed himself into this huddle of paramedics to give them another hand, forcing me to rise and step away from the patient.

The shrill, piercing voice of the man's wife filled the room. "Somebody do something, do something, please!"

The Zone Car announced its arrival over the air and requested our location.

I nodded at the captain, then approached the terror-stricken lady as he went outside to direct the paramedic lieutenant to the scene.

Now that there were five experts tending to the patient, I was able to concentrate my full attention to the frequently ignored family members.

"I want a doctor," she said, smoldering with hysteria. "Why aren't you all taking him to the hospital?"

I placed my left hand on her narrow right shoulder. "He needs emergency care this very moment."

"I want a doctor."

"He's getting the best medical treatment there is, ma'am. Please, you must believe me." She trembled. Her tearful eyes darted from me to her husband, then back to me. "A doctor would be performing the same medical procedures as these very qualified and capable men."

I withdrew my hand from her shoulder as she clutched the front of her bathrobe with her right hand. She wasn't listening. "I . . . I want a doctor."

"Ma'am. Even a doctor would have to do what they're doing right now. Please, believe me. He's getting the very best medical care."

The young woman released the lapel of her robe and began to wring her hands. She wanted to believe me. She was desperate for belief. "But . . . but why aren't they taking him to the hospital?"

"Because," I said calmly, "because he has a greater chance of survival if we treat him here—right now."

"Oh, God," she moaned.

"Mommy?"

I turned around and saw a pre-teenage girl in her pajamas standing at the entrance of the hallway.

"Tina." The lady rushed over to her daughter. "Sweetheart, go back to bed."

I heard McCormac say they had to intubate. They were seriously involved in a code red and doing everything humanly possible for Harry. I went over to his wife and child in an effort to shield them from the rough, but necessary, methods employed during a code: CPR, intubation of the airway, and defibrillation.

"Stop CPR. Clear the patient." McCormac hesitated. "Everybody clear?" Then he pressed the green button on the monitor and shocked the patient.

After a rhythm analysis and a vital signs assessment and a brief conference with the Zone Car lieutenant, he shocked the patient two more times. The poor cardiac response to the shocks confirmed the seriousness of this man's predicament.

I snapped out of my trance, caused by the dramatic defibrillation procedures, as soon as they resumed CPR and began pushing meds into the patient. When I turned around to address the mother, her daughter confronted me.

"What's wrong with my dad?"

"I . . . I'm—we're not sure."

The girl looked at her father. "Is my daddy going to be alright?"

I stepped in front of the girl to obstruct her view, as I calmly whispered to the mother. "Why don't you take her into your bedroom?"

The mother automatically responded to my suggestion. She took her daughter by the hand and led her across the living room.

I followed them down the hallway into the master bedroom and watched her direct her daughter to sit on the edge of the double bed.

"What am I going to do?" The mother turned to me. "What can I do?"

"Well, ahh . . . ahh . . . do you believe in prayer?" She vehemently nodded her head like a child. "Then . . . pray," I entreated, with sincerity. "Pray."

She knelt hard on the floor with her back to me and bowed her desperate angelic head. "Oh, please, God, p-l-e-a-s-e." She exhaled the last word with such breathy anguish that her daughter became less frightened by my strange presence in their bedroom than by the squeezed delivery of her mother's petition. As the intensity of the woman's prayer increased, her daughter knelt beside her and trembled.

I didn't know what else to do but maintain my tentative influence over them and listen to the boys work the hopeless code. After a while, I poked my head past the opened bedroom doorway and caught a glimpse of the captain standing in the living room near the mouth of the hallway. He winked at me to convey his approval over what I was doing.

"Which hospital?" I carefully projected down the hallway.

"Norfolk General. Get his I.D. from her."

"Right." I waited until the intensity of the wife's prayer digressed into silent tears and child-hugging before I interrupted her. "Ma'am. I hate to bother you, but we need your husband's driver's license and his insurance card."

The woman stood up, crossed the bedroom, and found her husband's wallet on top of their bureau. Her hands trembled as she rummaged through the wallet. As soon as she handed me the driver's license and insurance card, I left the room and glided down the hallway to give Ron the identification.

"Stay with her until we have him packaged and out of the house."

"I will." I went back to the bedroom and found the mother caressing her daughter. I waited a long time, until she stopped crying. "They're taking your husband to Norfolk General Hospital. Do you have someone you can call?"

She had to digest the inquiry. "Y-e-s. Yes. My brother."

"Good. Maybe you can ask him to drive you to the emergency room."

She forgot her daughter and hurried out of the bedroom to make the phone call. So, I escorted the girl to the living room where she scurried to her mother's side.

Fortunately, they had transported her husband out of the house. The lady had the telephone pressed hard against her ear; she waited intensely for her brother to answer the call.

"Are you alright?" I asked.

"Fine." She nodded mechanically. "Fine."

"He'll be at Norfolk General's Emergency Room," I repeated.

"Norfolk General." She nodded. "Emergency Room," she added. "Tim?" She burst into tears. "You've got to come over here, quick. Something terrible has happened to Harry. They're taking him to Norfolk General Hospital." Her daughter began to whimper as she listened to her mother explain the horrible circumstances to her brother.

There wasn't anything more I could do but back away from them and quietly shut the front door on my way out. By the time I reached the ambulance, they had the stretcher locked in place and they were shutting the rear door of the ambulance so it could proceed to the hospital.

I looked at Ric and the captain. "How does it look?"

Ric shook his head ominously.

"They're just going through the steps," said Ron.

"Protocol," Ric added.

"I thought so." I sighed. "Damn. He died right in front of me. I saw it. He imploded." I shook my head. "I knew he was dead."

"There's still hope," Ron said.

"You really think so?"

The silence between us was my answer.

We watched the ambulance drive away, then we shuffled back to the piece and climbed onboard.

Sensing our somber mood, Sam remained quiet. He turned off the emergency running lights, released the parking brakes, and slowly accelerated the engine as the captain keyed the radio.

"Engine Fifteen is in the clear."

"Ten-four, Engine Fifteen, at 0218. Run number, 14128."

"Ten-four."

We went straight to bed after we got back to the station, but I couldn't sleep. At two-thirty in the morning, I lay in my bed and stared into the darkness while Ric and Sam tossed and turned.

I made a conscious effort to forget our last incident.

29

THIRD-ALARM FIRE

RIC AND SAM MANAGED to achieve some degree of slumber, but I was still wide awake when the brass hit.

"Ten-one house fire, flames and smoke visible. Engine Fifteen respond to 2707 Pretty Lake Avenue on a report of a house fire. Flames and smoke visible. Time out: 0343."

I ran to the overhead door, pressed the button to raise it, and ran to my side of the piece to get into my boots and nightpants. By the time I reached for my turnout coat, I heard Ric and Sam hobbling toward the piece and I heard the captain responding to the dispatcher on his portable radio.

I got into my turnout coat, slammed my side-door closed, then ran to the apparatus door switch to wait for Sam to drive the piece onto the apron. By the time the engine rolled out of the station, I had my Nomex hood around my neck and tucked inside the collar of my buttoned turnout coat. I pressed the switch to close the door, ran to the idling piece, and slammed my side-door shut as soon as I climbed onboard.

"Let's go!" Ric hollered.

I sat in my jump seat to insert my arms through the SCBA tank straps as Sam floored the accelerator, which forced Ric, who was struggling into his turnout coat, to hold onto the back of his jump seat. The captain turned on the siren.

We knew this was a legitimate call and that we were first-in engine company.

Sam drove the piece as if he had bugs in his teeth. The captain was already communicating with the second-in engine company. Ric was cursing at a dropped smoke cutter as he was buttoning down. And I was mentally going over procedures as I was tightening my SCBA harness straps.

Radio chatter indicated that NPD was on the scene. They confirmed flames and heavy smoke at a small apartment complex surrounded by evacuated residents.

Sam took a right on Bay View Boulevard, a left on Cape View Avenue, and a right on East Ocean View Avenue where we raced toward Seventh Bay Street to take a hard right.

Once I settled into my gear, I grew calm. I glanced at Ric; he looked like a gladiator waiting to step into the arena.

This was the lull before the storm. The moment we lived for. This was when training and instinct, discipline and experience came together with a steady mind.

I loved it. God, I loved being close to the edge.

The streets were vacant. The noise of the siren and the radio, along with the sound of the engine's alternating acceleration and deceleration, accompanied by the flutter of the engaging jake-brake, was a constant. There was no future beyond our destination.

As soon as Sam rolled onto Seventh Bay, I unlatched a pick-head axe from the bulkhead in front of me and Ric grabbed the irons: a halligan tool married to a flathead axe by a Velcro strap wrapped midway around their handles.

The engine crossed Pleasant Avenue and continued along Seventh Bay to Pretty Lake Avenue, where we took a left and approached a three-story apartment complex on the right side of the street.

"Ric!"

"Yeah, Captain!"

"Take the pre-connected two-and-a-half off the rear hosebed!"

"Right!" Ric looked at me and smiled in triumph. "I guess it's on my side this time."

I displayed a "thumbs up" with my right hand. "Let's do it!"

We pulled our tanks out of their jump seat cradles and stood up as the captain keyed the radio.

"Engine Fifteen's on the scene. We have a three-story framed structure with flames and smoke visible. Engine Fifteen is in command." Then he directed incoming pieces, as well as requested additional engines, which made this a third-alarm fire.

Ric popped open his door and stepped down onto the street as soon as Sam stopped the engine and engaged the parking brakes. "There's heavy smoke on the second floor!"

I popped open my door as Sam placed the engine into pump gear. "Sam!"

"What!?"

"Hold off on the water until we get the line flaked out to the door!"

"Alright! But don't take too long!"

"We won't! Don't worry!"

By the time I reached the back of the piece, Ric had the nozzle and part of a long section pulled off the rear hosebed. He hoisted the forward end of the section over his shoulder, held onto the nozzle and the irons, and headed for the building with the rear of the hoisted section dragging behind him.

I laid my axe on the ground, climbed onto the tailboard, and payed-out a section of line to help Ric's progress. Then I grabbed a partial section of hoseline and pulled it off the bed, hoisted the front end to my shoulder and headed in Ric's direction with the bundle dragging behind me and the line paying-out of the rear of the engine's hosebed. The captain took my place on the tailboard and continued paying-out the remaining sections from the hosebed to help my progress to the apartment building; I knew he would clear the hosebed, then serve as my backup on this heavy line.

Ric had the line payed-off his back by the time he climbed the stairs and reached the second floor. He was able to get the line to the door, which was not far from the stairwell, because of my advance.

Heavy smoke poured out of the apartment's opened door.

After I reached the second floor, I continued up the stairs to the third floor, then I flaked the line off my back on my way down the stairwell to the second floor. Without the captain providing me slack, I couldn't have laid the line in this manner so that, once it was charged with water, its weight going down the stairs as we hauled on the line, would assist us in our advances deep into the apartment to attack the seat of the fire.

On my way to Ric, I saw the captain in the parking lot below. I leaned over the banister from the building's open hallway on the second floor. "Captain! Tell Sam to give us water!"

Ron acknowledged my request with a single wave, then he shouted back, "Everybody's out of the apartment!"

I approached Ric and knelt down beside him on the cement floor. "You hear that, Ric?"

"What?"

"Everybody's out."

"Thank God." He grinned. "I reckon there's nothin' left for us to do but knock down this fire."

"I reckon."

"Where's the water?"

"It's coming," I said.

We donned our masks, turned on our air, raised our Nomex hoods, tightened our helmet chin-straps, raised and Velcroed our coat collars, and slipped on our gloves.

Ric grabbed the nozzle of the uncharged line and leaned against the wall near the doorway beside me. We watched the black smoke pour out into the second-floor breezeway until the line tightened with water. Ric cracked open the nozzle, bled the charged line, and adjusted the nozzle setting while I grabbed hold of the line several feet behind him as his backup.

Ric shut the nozzle. "Ready!?"

"Let's go!"

We stood up and shuffled in front of the door. An interior explosion caused us to crouch involuntarily.

No telling what that was, I thought. An aerosol or paint can— something.

The captain approached us from behind. "Be careful!" Then he threw his helmet back, letting it hang on his neck by the chin-strap, and donned his facemask and hood.

Ric and I walked inside and saw the orange fire glowing deep within the darkness of what must have been the living room. Ric opened the nozzle, as we advanced toward the orange glow, and directed the water stream on the fire.

The room blackened and the heat increased and almost pushed us back with its intensity. We knelt on the floor and hunched forward, while struggling to keep the water stream directed toward the fire, to let the steamed heat pass over us. The fire flared ferociously.

I held my position behind Ric as he continued to direct the water stream at the blaze until the glow went out. Then we stood up and advanced the line toward what must have been the entrance of the kitchen and the entrance to the nearby hallway.

Because the space surrounding us was pitch black, guessing and instinct and experience was what we had to operate with as we advanced deeper into the apartment. Knowing when the environment was becoming too dangerous came with experience. Yet getting caught in a flashback or in a flashover was still a threat with veteran fire fighters, since they had a habit of forging ahead despite the intense heat.

When the line became easier to advance, I knew the captain was feeding it to us at the apartment's entrance. This allowed him to maintain a measure of command and control of the fireground, as well as maintain direct communication with us while providing backup manpower support.

The kitchen was fully involved and a series of small explosions made Ric and I flinch as we entered the small space and attacked the fire.

Aerosol spray cans exploded. Glass shattered. Objects fell and broke. Things popped in the dark.

We knocked down most of the fire, then backed out of the kitchen and stumbled toward the hallway and into the captain, who had followed the line inside to assist us after the battalion chief had relieved him of the fireground command. He remained third man on the line and followed us further into the apartment.

The orange glow of the fire gave us our only directional point of reference. As we fought fire down the hallway, part of the ceiling came down and exposed an inferno in the cockloft. Ric directed the water stream up into the attic cockloft and held it steady for a long time. When the fire above remained unaffected by the water from our line, it became apparent to me that the building was constructed with an open cockloft, which extended the entire length of the structure. If the building was to be saved, the roof had to be ventilated and several more lines had to be employed: one at each end of the cockloft, a line behind the building, a backup line following us inside, and several other lines deployed where needed for exposures. Until there was enough water directed against this fire to put it out, all we could do was fight the fire we had until our tank bells began to ring, telling us we were running out of air.

The fire finally began to dampen a bit, so Ric decided to shut down the line and advance along the hallway to the nearest bedroom. When Ric reached the first door, he found it closed and had to feel for the doorknob. To our utter surprise, the room was fully involved when he pushed the door open. He opened the nozzle and directed the water stream into the bedroom for a long while, as he stood at the door's threshold. Then he advanced into the bedroom, with me supporting the line behind him, which Ron was feeding to me.

The ceiling of the bedroom was already down and there was fire above us and on two sides. Ric directed the stream onto the most intense area until it posed a lesser threat, then moved on to the next most intense blaze, until the fire was knocked down.

Suddenly, I heard Ric's muffled holler. When I felt the line dip to the ground, I knew Ric had fallen. I barely understood Ric through his facepiece, and I knew he was having difficulty understanding me.

"Ric! Ric! Are you alright!?"

I heard Ric shut down the line. "My leg! My leg!"

I leaned toward him and grabbed a hold of the top of his SCBA tank.

"What's wrong!? What's wrong!?"

"My leg! My leg went through the floor!"

I heard the muffle of the captain's voice and translated it to be, "What's wrong?"

I leaned closer to Ric, having to ignore the captain, so I could understand the muffled voice behind Ric's facemask, as well as make my own muffled voice clearer to him.

"Is it broke!?"

"No! Just caught!"

"I'll help you up!" I hooked my right arm under his right armpit and grabbed the top of his tank harness with my left hand. "Ready!?"

"Yeah!"

I straightened up, pulling him with me. He leaned to his right, indicating his effort to rise up, using his right leg. After he was standing, I felt him yank his left foot out of the hole in the floor. Our tanks' bells began to ring.

"Can you walk!?"

"I'm fine!"

I felt the captain pull on my tank. Then I heard him ask, "What's wrong!?"

"Ric! Ric's foot went through the floor! He's alright!"

"Is he alright!?"

"He's—all—right!"

Ric picked up the nozzle. "Just another minute!" Ric directed the line to the cockloft and opened the nozzle. After the fire in the loft seemed to dampen, the captain insisted that it was time to leave.

We backed out of the bedroom with the hoseline, laid the nozzle and the line in the hallway, and followed the two-and-a-half to the outside of the apartment where another fire company was preparing to enter.

I threw back my helmet and it hung from my neck by its chinstrap, pulled down my Nomex hood, and tore my mask away from my face. What was left of my air escaped noisily through the low pressure hose of my detached mask.

The captain tore off his mask, anxious to brief the company preparing to go in. "The nozzle is in the hallway. We knocked down the fire in the living room, kitchen, and first bedroom. Be careful. The other bedrooms may be fully involved. The cockloft is fully involved. The ceiling is coming down. Ric's leg went through the floor."

The men listened as they finished tanking up, then they followed the line into the apartment and disappeared into the black.

"Look out!" Ric said. "We kicked hell out of that fire, don't you think, Captain?"

"Good job," said Ron, displaying a grin. "You all did a good job."

Both sides of their faces were black like I knew mine must have been.

"Who—yaa!" I hollered, adrenalin still coursing through my body. "I think we earned our pay tonight, don't you?"

"The night ain't over yet," said Ric.

"He's right about that," said the captain. "Let's change these tanks and take a break. From the looks of this fire, we may have to go back in."

"Do you think so?" I said.

"Maybe."

"Don't worry," said Ric, as he led the way down the stairs. "I believe we're going to find out."

We did go back inside later and fight more fire. Then we helped overhaul the building until the C-shift relieved us on-station that morning.

30

HARD SLEEPLESS NIGHT

AT SEVEN-FIFTEEN in the morning, the parking lot and the street at 2707 Pretty Lake Avenue was still crowded with a variety of fire suppression vehicles: engines and ladders, a squad and a rescue unit, arson and police sedans, safety and media vans, and numerous chief cars and SUVs representing upper level departmental management—the director, the fire chief, the shift commander. At this late stage, there were more people at the scene than were necessary and more people standing around than working.

The noise of idling vehicles permeated the atmosphere, and the presence of fire-gear cluttered the area: strewn turnout coats, gloves, and helmets; discarded hand tools and portable power equipment; unattended hoselines, forming an unintended visual abstraction created by a spaghetti weave of five-inch, two-and-a-half-inch, and inch-and-a-half hoselines running off of engine hosebeds toward and around and inside the building on all three levels.

Overhaul had been a tedious affair of pulling down ceilings, destRicing walls, flooding spaces, taking out insulation, and drenching smoldering beams and voids, as well as rooms and attic spaces throughout the building. The long overhaul period had dampened all the glory of our aggressive attack earlier that morning, leaving us exhausted.

I sat beside Ric on the tailboard of our engine to wait for our reliefs. Ron was inspecting the inside of the building with the battalion chief and shift commander. And Sam was killing time cavorting with another engine driver. By the time C-shift arrived in Bobby Guenther's pickup truck, we were feeling washed out and humorless and anxious to get back to the station to get cleaned up and go home.

"Where's the captain?" Bobby demanded, as he got out of his truck with Doug and tossed Ric the keys.

"Inside," I said. "With the battalion chief and shift commander."

"Looks like you all had a good one," said Doug, who was Engine Fifteen's driver on the C-shift.

"Yeah, we burned another one down," Ric retorted, prepared for a gibe that did not come. "Where's your captain?"

"He tapped out this morning," said Bobby. "I've got the company today. We would have been here sooner, but we had to wait for two fill-ins."

"Damn," I said. "Where'd everybody go?"

"Tom's on furlough and Pete's got the Kelly day."

"Hell of a good day for a Kelly," said Ric.

"Amen to that, brother." Bobby pointed at two guys disembarking from the bed of his pickup truck. "But look what they sent me from Seven and Thirteen."

"Lord, God, is that you, Dinkens?" Sam interjected, as he approached us.

"Hello there, big boy," Dinkens hailed, as he confronted Sam and shook hands with him.

"If your head gets any bigger," Sam teased, "Firebrand is gonna have to design you a special helmet."

"Haw, haw. You're just jealous."

"Who's that with you, Dinkens?" I interrupted.

"One of our C-shift rookies."

"Hey there, rookie. I'm Danny."

The young fire fighter smiled broadly, expressing his genuine delight to be here. "Hey! I'm Beck."

"Hello, Beck."

Bobby surveyed the building. "Where inside do you reckon the captain is?"

I pointed to one of the doors on the second floor. "In there."

"Alright. I'll get him out of there so you all can go home."

"I'll leave your truck keys in the captain's middle desk drawer," said Ric.

"Alright." Bobby turned away from us and headed for the building to relieve our captain.

We gathered our turnout gear and personal items from the engine, after we stripped out of our nightpants and fire boots, and loaded our stuff into the back of Bobby's pickup. Then Ric got behind the wheel of the truck, while Sam and I climbed into the bed of the pickup, knowing we didn't have long to wait.

"Here he comes now," said Ric. "And look at him hustle."

"That captain still has a lot of private in him," I said.

"Amen to that," said Sam.

The captain stopped at the piece to get his own personal gear out of the cab, then scurried to Bobby's truck. He hesitated beside the awaiting vehicle to draw greater attention. "What the hell are we waiting for?"

Ric started the truck. "Would you please get your sorry butt into this truck, Captain?"

Everybody laughed.

"Get in, Ron," I said, "before Ric goes off on you."

He tossed me his turnout coat and helmet. "Good job, you all." Then he opened the truck's passenger door. "Fresh pot's on me." He got into the cab, slammed the door shut, and urged Ric to step on the gas.

The road wind felt great as we rolled along Seventh Bay away from the fire scene and toward our day off, which was already marred by fatigue and hunger and coffee deprivation. Many fire fighters worked a part-time day job when off-duty. But after a hard sleepless night, topped off by a working fire until morning lineup, even the hardiest souls sometimes went home to rest instead of trying to earn a few more dollars to support their families.

Ric drove to the back of the station and parked the vehicle in front of the rear apparatus door. Sam and I threw everybody's gear out of the truck's bed, as the captain entered the station through the side-door and hit the switch to open the rear overhead door. Then he returned to the truck to retrieve his gear with the rest of us.

We dispersed—each of us taking care of our personal needs, according to our individual priorities. Ron went into the galley to start a pot of coffee. Ric backed Bobby's truck into a proper parking spot. Sam went into the barracks-side bathroom to get cleaned up. And I went into the watchroom to reset the monitor. Ric and I converged in the locker room; we heard Sam flush one of the toilets.

"Damn, brother," Ric gibed. "I think we used the wrong hose to stop that fire."

Sam entered the locker room, displaying a timid grin. "Yeah." Then he began taking off his clothes in front of his locker.

"You workin' your part-time job today?" Ric prodded.

"I'm gonna try."

"Damn." Ric clucked twice at him, then glanced at me after a realization. "That's right. This here young'n is still in his twenties."

Sam piled his dirty clothes on the floor, snatched his towel from the makeshift hook made from a wire hanger that was attached to the front vent of his locker door, and went back into the bathroom.

"You can't get to him," I said.

Ric shrugged his shoulders and chuckled. "I know it."

I chose to strip off my dirty t-shirt and wash up at the sink, after I answered nature's call. I decided to take a shower after I got home.

After I was reasonably clean, I went back to my locker, found a clean t-shirt, and put it on as I went into the barracks bedroom to strip my bed. Ric entered the bedroom as I was folding my sheets and blanket.

"I don't know why I bothered to make mine yesterday," he said. "I don't think I spent an hour in it."

"Yeah." I placed my pillow on top of my folded blanket and linen, then plopped face down on the bare mattress. "This day doesn't stand a chance."

Ric sighed. "I know. Kick the dog or kick the wife—either way, you lose." He stripped his rack and gathered his linen into a wad rather than fold it.

The captain keyed the station's intercom. "Fresh pot! Fresh pot!"

"Come on, big boy. Let's go to the galley for some coffee and talk trash."

I lifted my head from the mattress. "Go on. I'll be in there in a minute." I plopped my head back down and watched Ric saunter into the locker room, where Sam was standing naked as a jaybird.

Ric whistled. "Lord, God, you're a pretty sight!"

I rolled over on my back and chuckled. I liked this blue-collar world of ordinary exceptional men. I closed my eyes and drifted into the comfort of the barrack's bedroom security, as I listened to the friendly antics of two fire fighters I deeply respected.

31

FILL IN THE HOLES

I was hovering over my second cup of coffee and listening to the crisp banter between Sam and Ric when T. C. arrived from his fill-in at Station Eight to drop off his turnout gear on his way home. The animated, brotherly attitude at the table flattened.

"Hey, T. C.," I said. "How was your fill-in?"

His facial expression conveyed that it had been difficult, but he said, "It was alright. We were up all night on medical calls."

"We were up all night, too," I said.

"I know. I heard you all go out on the air."

Sam rose and went to the sink. "Yeah, you missed a good one." He washed out his cup. "You might have learned something if you'd have been there."

"That's for sure," Ric added.

"He's got plenty of time to get fireground experience," I said, in his defense.

"Damn near twenty-five years," Ric taunted.

T. C. smiled uneasily. "I'm not worried. I'm in no rush."

Sam placed his clean cup in the drainboard. "Yeah." The tone in his voice suggested that he should be.

T. C. sat at the table across from me and quietly watched Sam leave the galley. "Where's the captain?"

"He's in his office working on his fire report," I said.

Ric stretched. "Well, I reckon it's time for me to go." He rose, laid his cup in the sink, and patted my back on his way out. "See you next day."

"Later, brother," I said. I winked at our rookie, T. C. "Don't pay any attention to them."

"That's easy for you to say."

I drank some of my coffee. "You really did miss a good one."

"I couldn't help that," he said defensively.

"Hey, don't get me wrong. I didn't mean that in a bad way."

"Oh, I know, I know. And I didn't mean to sound so, well . . . ." He pursed his lips, then pondered for a few moments. "What's wrong with those boys?"

"Nothing."

"I don't think they like me. What have I done?"

"Nothing. You've done nothing wrong that experience won't take care of."

"I don't understand."

"Well—I think they're misinterpreting your inexperience with laziness and with what appears to be a lack of effort on the fire-ground."

"I do things!" he said.

"I know, I know, but . . . ."

"But what?"

"What I've seen, and you've got to understand that I'm trying to help you here—"

"I'm listening."

"Well—you do what you're told."

"I do. I really do."

"Yeah. But only what you're told to do. And that's the point. You're always waiting to be told."

"Huh?"

"Yeah. That's it. You've got to learn how to fill in the holes."

"What holes?"

"I've told you about this."

"I know, but—"

"It's the job that needs to be done next. The end that needs to be lifted when the other end is picked up by another fire fighter. This job is a company effort. If you see somebody dragging a line, you need to back him up. If hoseline is being taken up, you need to pitch in and help break the couplings and drain the sections and roll the dirty hose and even climb into another engine's hosebed to help them pack. If we stop at a hydrant to top off our engine's tank and you see your partner grab the hydrant wrench, then you should get the fill hose. If your partner is the nozzle man, then you're his backup. If your partner grabs a pike pole, you grab a pick-head axe. Whatever your partner is doing, you have to find the task that supports him. You've got to see the bigger picture to every fireground task. If I'm told to get a ladder off the piece, you need to come along with me to carry one end. You see? You've got to fill in the hole. You've got to watch what your partner is doing, listen to the captain's orders, and understand what needs to be done to complete a fireground task."

"But a lot of times I don't know."

"Then watch and learn from the veterans. See what they do. It won't take you long to learn."

"I'll learn. I swear, I'll learn."

"I know you will. But you'll have to hustle. Because, you see, the real trick is to initiate the task so that your partner has to fill in the hole. This doesn't mean that you're competing with him. This simply makes you an aggressive fire fighter on the fireground. And that's the kind of reputation you want. If you're aggressive with the little things, believe me, you'll be aggressive with the bigger and more dangerous things, like fighting that fire dragon when you go in."

T. C. frowned. "Little things, huh?"

"That's right."

"I'm not afraid to work hard. But sometimes . . . sometimes I don't know what to do."

"I know that. And they know that. And that's alright. But sometimes, and I've seen it, your confusion registers on your face as a scowl when you're told to do something—like you did a second ago."

"I didn't mean nothin'."

"I know that."

"It's my face."

"Sure. But you've got to erase your face."

"What?"

"Yeah. You need to erase your facial expressions on the fireground, especially when you're assigned a menial task. Because there are no menial tasks on the fireground, especially for a rookie."

"Damn. I see."

"Everybody notices, what appears to be, a bad attitude. There are no secrets on the fireground. Word gets around fast in this department. And once you get a bad reputation, it's hard to raise yourself up again. The best rep you can get is 'he's a damn good fire fighter.' That equalizes everything else, including being an outsider or having an odd personality."

"I'm just quiet."

"I wasn't accusing you of being anything. I'm just saying this: be an aggressive, hard-working fire fighter on the fireground, and you're automatically one of the boys—no matter who you are. Got it?"

T. C. bowed his head thoughtfully. "Yeah."

"You okay?"

He nodded. "I've got to be."

"Don't worry," I said. "You'll be alright."

He shook his head. "This is a hard place."

I stood up and I chuckled. "You've got that right. People. That's the hardest part of any job. We're our own worse enemy." I went to the sink, washed out my cup, and set it in the drainboard before turning to T. C. "When I was a rookie, an old-timer told me, 'A fire fighter is the dumbest animal on this planet. He knows he's risking his life for low wages, but he does it anyway. He knows the city will try to kick him to the curb when he gets hurt and can't work, but he stays with the job anyway.' " I smiled to imitate the old-timer's transition into pride. " 'And because he's a special breed of animal, he can't help himself.' " As I walked out, I tapped T. C.'s shoulder. "You'll be alright. Count on me to help you, anytime."

"Later, man."

"Yeah." I crossed the apparatus floor and went into the captain's office. Ron was on the computer, completing his fire report. "You still here?"

"Uh-huh." He continued typing. "I'm about done. Had to catch up on my other reports, as well as the daily report."

"Yuck." I looked over his shoulder at the screen. In the Method of Extinguishment box, he checked number six: pre-connect hose/hydrant. In the Level of Fire Origin box, he checked number four: 30 to 49 feet. And when he arrived at the Estimated Total Dollar Loss box, he hesitated.

"What do you think, Danny?"

"Hell, your guess is as good as mine." I nudged him with the heel of my hand. "That's why you get the big captain bucks." He chuckled. "I'm out of here."

"See you tomorrow," he said, without looking away from the computer screen.

I walked out of the office and went to the locker room to get my station-bag and dirty t-shirt and lock my locker. Then I walked the length of the empty apparatus floor out to the rear parking lot, threw my stuff into the trunk of my vehicle before getting behind the wheel, started the car, and drove out of the parking lot to head home on a day that started at three-forty-three in the morning—wait, no—at one-thirteen in the morning.

"Whoa," I sighed. I was looking forward to a nap when I got home.

32

I'LL TAKE CARE OF DANA

I OPENED MY EYES and saw my wife standing beside my bed.

"Hi, honey," she whispered. "Are you alright?"

"Yeah." I blinked my eyes, sat up, and indicated that I wanted a kiss. She responded with a hug as well. "Have you been here long?"

"Just got here. I didn't wake you, did I?"

"No." I yawned. "Short nap. Long dream."

"Good or bad?"

"I don't know."

"Where's Kevin?"

"You mean, he's not here?" I glanced at his empty bed. "Hmmm. He must be roaming the hallways." I smiled. "A nurse will be escorting him back into the room shortly."

"Poor baby. Here you are in the hospital and stuck in a room with a crazy man."

"Yeah, well, he's alright. He's harmless, despite his condition, you know . . . ."

"Korsakoff's Syndrome."

"Right. He's as considerate as he's able to be. He grows on you. In fact, I kind of like him."

She laid an affectionate hand on my forearm. "That's just like you to overlook a difficult situation."

"I have no choice."

"But you do it so well."

"I don't know about that."

"I love you, sweetheart."

"I love you, too."

"You're going to be alright."

"I know." I patted her hand. "I know." I didn't want to worry her. "How's your writing coming along?"

"Slow. Hard. This book is going to be eight hundred pages long, if I don't watch out."

"Don't worry about the length. Just write the book. The length will take care of itself."

"I hope so. I want the book to flow. I want it to get published."

"You're a great writer. It flows. And you're a great philosopher. Just write the book and worry about getting it published later."

She told me more about how her work was developing and she told me how many more books she needed to read. I listened to her and encouraged her and loved her for being the very special lady I'd been married to for thirty years. Then Kevin made his entrance, escorted by the head nurse.

"I almost made it to the bar, Dana."

"You did?"

Paranoia assaulted him. "Don't worry, man, I would have brought you a beer."

"Oh, I know that."

"You get into bed and behave," the nurse said to him, as she winked at me. She left the room after he sat on the edge of his bed.

"Hello, Kevin," said Kathleen.

Kevin waved at her. "Can you believe the way they treat a grown man?"

"She's trying to take care of you."

"Yeah, yeah, I guess. Like a monkey in a cage."

She grinned at me.

"Well, hon," I said, "there's no use in your hanging around here."

"I don't mind."

I pulled her closer to me and whispered into her ear. "With Kevin here, we won't get any time together. Go home. And call my parents again to let them know that I'm still doing fine, okay?"

"Are you sure?"

"Go home." I kissed her. She kissed me back. "I love you."

"I love you, too." She picked up her purse. "Bye, Kevin."

"Bye, bye. And don't worry. I'll take care of Dana for you."

"Thank you." She sighed for my sake. "I'm sure you will."

33

FALSE ALARM

AFTER A LONG EVENING with Kevin, I managed to get him to turn off the lights so I could go to sleep. Shortly thereafter, I was disturbed by a nurse, who gave me medication. Then I was aroused by a hospital attendant so she could take my vital signs.

Falling asleep was a hopeless endeavor, but I struggled toward the edge of slumber anyway.

The brass hit.

"Fire alarm. Engine Fifteen respond to 812 Widgeon Road on a report of a fire alarm. Time out: 0348."

I struggled out of my rack, feeling brain dead, and almost lost my balance getting into my trousers. When I glanced at the other beds, I noticed neither Ric nor Sam were stirring from their racks. "Sam! Get up! Ric! Come on, we've got a run!"

Sam raised his head from under his blanket, looking like a turtle poking its head out of its shell. "What?"

"We've got a run!"

"God," said Ric, as he flipped his linen aside and rolled out of bed.

They started hustling into their pants by the time I reached the door leading to the apparatus floor. After checking their progress, I pushed through the double door and shuffled past the engine to the overhead door, pressed the switch to raise it, and went to my side of the piece to put on my nightpants and fireboots. By the time I got my suspenders over my shoulders, I heard the boys approaching the engine. Neither one of them were moving very quickly.

Ric climbed onboard, sat down, and slammed his side-door shut, not bothering to get into any of his gear. Then he rested his head against the door with his eyes closed, figuring that this was a false alarm. Sam seemed to have trouble climbing onboard, then he seemed to have trouble starting the engine. When I realized that the captain hadn't joined us yet, I dashed into his office and went to his bedroom. He was sound asleep.

"Ron. Ron!"

He stirred in his bed. He sat up. He shook his head.

"We've got a run! Come on!"

"Jesus!" He grabbed his portable radio and followed me out to the apparatus floor without putting on his pants or shoes. "Get on the piece," he said to me. "Leave the apparatus door open." Then he slipped on his nightpants and boots, that were sitting on the floor near the right front wheel of the piece, and climbed into the idling engine as I slammed my door shut and sat down.

"Let's go!" said the captain.

Sam rolled onto the apron and took a left on Fishermans Road, then suddenly decelerated.

"What's wrong?" the captain demanded.

"Where are we going?"

"Shoot! Where are we going?" the captain repeated.

"Eight-twelve Widgeon Road!" I yelled. "On a fire alarm!"

Sam accelerated the engine, then decelerated. "Christ. Widgeon. Where's Widgeon Road, Captain?"

"You know, Widgeon! You know where Widgeon is!"

"A blank, Captain. I'm drawing a blank. Which way is it?"

The captain drew a blank, as well, and called out to Ric and me. "Where's Widgeon Road!?"

Ric and I didn't answer. We looked at each other with blank, brain-dead expressions.

"Engine Fifteen, dispatcher. Are you responding?"

"Damn!" The captain keyed the radio. "Engine Fifteen's responding."

"Ten-four, Engine Fifteen."

"Where's Widgeon Road?" the captain repeated to everybody on the piece, as Sam kept driving slowly toward Chesapeake Boulevard.

"Check the map book, Captain!" I finally said.

This ridiculously obvious suggestion concerning the application of a routine activity stunned the captain, momentarily, before he took action. He fumbled with the map book. His mental faculties were not engaged any better than the driver's.

Sam was operating on subconscious autopilot; when we reached Chesapeake Boulevard, he crossed the main thoroughfare and continued to Old Ocean View Boulevard, where he took a left.

"Hit the siren, Captain!" I shouted.

"Right!"

Then I noticed Sam turning on the running lights. Sam was driving the engine at full speed and not his usual hard speed. He wasn't sure where he was going, but he was going.

"Widgeon! It's off of Tidewater Drive!" the captain disclosed.

The engine's speed suddenly increased. That sparse piece of information jarred something inside of Sam; at least, I hoped it did. I know I was having a difficult time without having to drive or having to deal with the dispatcher or having to know where we were going.

"Engine Nine is on the scene."

"Ten-four, Engine Nine."

"Ladder Nine is on the scene."

"Ten-four, Ladder Nine."

Sam swerved to his right to avoid an oncoming car; his driving skills were not as crisp as usual. When we reached Little Creek Road, he was less cautious in his right turn and outright dangerous in making a left, against a red traffic light, onto Tidewater Drive, where he didn't wait for the sparse oncoming traffic to slow down. The captain didn't seem to notice and Ric's eyes were closed again and I felt too numb to care.

"Battalion Two is on the scene."

"Ten-four, Battalion Two."

I finally recalled that Widgeon Road was quite a long southerly distance down the Tidewater Drive straightaway; I hoped the dispatcher cleared us before we arrived on the scene. We had no business being on the road in our hazy mental conditions. And if the citizens had any idea how dangerous it was to be anywhere near this engine right now, they would screech off the road into the safety of any parking lot until we passed by.

"Engine Nine, dispatcher."

"Engine Nine, go ahead."

"Clear all units with the exception of Engine Nine."

The captain turned off the siren. Sam decelerated the engine.

"Ten-four, Engine Nine. Clear all units responding to 812 Widgeon Road with the exception of Engine Nine."

Sam turned off the emergency running lights.

The captain switched back to Channel One and keyed the radio. "Engine Fifteen's in the clear."

"Ten-four, Engine Fifteen."

The four of us shared an inaudible sigh of relief as Sam pulled into a parking lot and made a U-turn back onto Tidewater Drive, going in the opposite direction, toward our station.

Ric opened his eyes, glanced at me, and whispered, "We were screwed up."

"You've got that right." I leaned against my door and closed my eyes, feeling grateful that this was a false alarm.

Finding the apparatus door still open when we got back to the station was a testament to our ragged mental condition. Sam slowly backed the engine into the station as if it were a damaged ship limping into a safe harbor after a terrible storm.

The captain keyed the radio. "Engine Fifteen's in quarters."

"Ten-four, Engine Fifteen."

Sam set the parking brakes, then killed the engine. The four of us remained seated and mute and as hollow as our surrounding silence. Ric broke the spell when he pulled the latch on his side-door and let the door swing open. He stepped heavily down from the piece and went to the watchroom to reset the monitor.

As I stepped out of the engine through Ric's door, Sam and Ron pulled their latches to release their doors. Sam slid out of the cab as I went into the bathroom to relieve myself.

When I was a rookie, an old-timer told me that a fire fighter should always relieve himself after every run, with or without the urge. He also advised me that a fire fighter should do so every time he woke up in the middle of the night because, once the brass hits, a fire fighter didn't know when he would have another opportunity to empty his bladder.

Sam shuffled into the bathroom and stepped into the other stall.

There were two toilet stalls without doors, three sinks, and one small shower in the green- and-white-tiled bathroom situated between the barracks bedroom and the locker room.

"You alright?" I delved carefully.

"Yeah."

Ric straggled into the bathroom after I flushed the toilet. I approached one of the sinks to wash my hands, as Ric went past me to occupy the vacated stall. Sam flushed his toilet as I was drying my hands with a paper towel. Then he went to a sink to wash his hands as I threw the wet paper towel into the trash and headed for the bedroom. I heard Ric flush his toilet as I was taking my pants off in the dark bedroom.

Whenever the brass hits, the monitor kicks on the lights and directs the dispatcher's voice into the speakers throughout the station. And whenever the monitor is reset, all the speakers throughout the station go off, except for the one in the watchroom; and all the lights in the station go out, except for the working lights on the apparatus floor as well as the lights that have been manually switched on.

Sam was shuffling to his bed and Ric was washing his hands by the time I was underneath my sheet and blanket. Light from the bathroom and locker room spilled through the open door leading into the bedroom.

After Ric finished drying his hands, he switched off the lights in the bathroom and the locker room, and shut the bedroom door behind him on his way to bed. Sam stretched underneath his blanket and exhaled deeply, as Ric approached his bed, took off his pants, and draped them over the back of a chair.

Ric exhaled as soon as his head hit the pillow. "You alright, Sam?"

"I am, now," Sam muttered.

"I'm sure glad you were driving," I said. "I was pretty screwed up on that last run."

"The captain wasn't much better off," Ric qualified.

Sam laughed. "He was downright messed up."

I chuckled. Ric giggled.

"He was the last one up after the brass," I said. "You should have seen him."

"We did!" Ric croaked. "When he stumbled into the apparatus floor in his skivvies and socks lookin' like a crazy man, Lord, I almost lost it."

Sam hooted. "I was so numb, I didn't see nothin'."

"Shoot," Ric added, "I had to close my eyes."

"Lord, God," I said. "I hope we have a quiet night."

"Amen to that, brother," said Ric. "What's left of it."

"Widgeon Road. I can't believe I had trouble with Widgeon Road."

"Goes to show you," Ric said, philosophically.

"What?" I said.

"Anytime you think you've got this job figured out, something will happen to make you eat humble pie."

"Yeah. You've got that right," Sam mumbled.

I heard Ric roll onto his side. "Damn. This night ain't gettin' any younger."

"Past four o'clock," I said.

"Near time to get up," said Sam.

"Damn farmer," Ric remarked.

"City boy," Sam countered.

"Hush. Both of you. I'm trying to get some sleep."

Silence prevailed, but slumber eluded all three of us with a terrible case of restlessness. After three quarters of an hour, I heard Sam get out of bed and put on his pants, then watched him leave the bedroom.

Ric sighed.

"You can't sleep either?" I murmured.

"Hell, no." Ric sat up. "And I've got to work my part-time job today."

I got out of bed and put on my pants. "Might as well get up. Come on. I'll buy you coffee."

Ric reached for his pants. "Sam's probably makin' some right now."

"Come on," I said, mischievously. "Let's grab the morning paper before he gets to it."

"Alright." Ric buckled his belt. "Let's do it."

We scurried out of the bedroom, crossed the apparatus floor into the galley, and discovered Sam and the captain at the table drinking coffee and reading the newspaper.

"Damn," said Ric. "How long have you been up, Captain?"

"I never went to sleep." He looked up from his newspaper. "That last run rattled me to the bone."

"I reckon it rattled all of us," Ric said, as he went to the cupboard, took out two coffee mugs, and handed me one.

I reached for the pot and poured him coffee. "I guess it could have been worse." I poured myself coffee.

"I guess." Ron looked down and gazed at the section of newspaper that lay spread before him.

I took a careful sip of my coffee, sat down beside Ric, and stared.

34

TRAGIC

"Good morning, Dana."

I shifted my blank gaze to Kevin, who was standing at my bedside. He was wearing a red t-shirt, a grey pair of sweatpants, a pair of blown-out sneakers, a baseball cap, and a calculating expression on his face.

"What."

"Are you ready?" he said.

"For what?"

"To bust out of here."

I stretched. I felt pain in my chest. "Kevin, Kevin." I forced a smile. I was too groggy to think of anything clever to say. "Let's wait for breakfast first."

"Screw breakfast. I'll buy you something to eat as soon as we're out of here."

"With what?"

Kevin tried to reach into a back pocket that wasn't there. "What? Where's my wallet?" Paranoia struck him. "Somebody stole my wallet, Dana."

"See what I mean?"

"This is serious, man."

"You don't have to convince me of that."

"Stay where you are." Kevin went to his bedside table and started rummaging through its drawers.

I got out of bed and went to the bathroom. With some difficulty, I changed my hospital gown and boxer shorts, brushed my teeth, washed my face, and shaved. The plastic, rectangular heart monitor, which dangled from a set of leads taped to my chest, was a nuisance. I had to adjust the relatively heavy portable monitor numerous times to prevent it from falling through the waistband of my boxer shorts.

I looked into the bathroom mirror and saw the imperceptible change in myself that only I could have seen. I rested both hands on the sink and carefully leaned closer to my image.

The eyes. They seemed emptier, less charged, darkened by fatigue and concern.

I had been in this hospital since Friday night, or rather, since early Saturday morning, and . . . well, here it was only Sunday morning and I felt I'd been here for a lifetime.

I looked away from the mirror, but kept my hands on the sink for support.

I had to remain optimistic. Things could have been worse. I could have had a major stroke. I could have been left paralyzed. I could have died.

I felt the monitor slipping down the elastic waistband of my boxer shorts. I adjusted it with my left hand. When I heard Kevin laugh, I sat down on the edge of the toilet; I needed a few additional moments of privacy.

Kevin was actually a very nice guy, but the constant chatter of his relentless external monologue was unnerving at times. Occasionally, I managed to divert him into silence, but the respite was never enough. Nevertheless, I couldn't get angry at him because he often penetrated the silence with an element of wisdom. Amazing.

I heard him slam a drawer shut. He was still searching for his wallet. Or his socks. Or for something he was unable to reveal to anybody. Tragic.

I sighed. Then I stood up, stepped toward the closed door, and reached for the knob. I hesitated.

Tomorrow. What will it bring? A new beginning? Or the end to the precious balance in my life. It rankled me to think that someone was going to run a wire through one of my blood vessels into my heart.

Damn. I wished I was home, or at work. But today was all I had, and today was a long way from tomorrow.

I chuckled.

Kevin would see to that.

I opened the bathroom door. "Did you find it?"

Kevin was on his knees, searching underneath his bed. He straightened up and looked at me. "Find what?"

"Your wallet?"

His eyes widened. "Nobody finds a stolen wallet."

"Then I guess we're stuck here."

"Not if I can find my keys."

"To what?"

He grimaced. "To the door."

"What door?"

He pointed to our room's closed door. "The door."

"That door isn't locked."

Kevin froze. "It isn't?"

I went to the door and opened it. "See?" Then I shut it.

"You're amazing, Dana. How'd you do that?" He grinned. "Are you a safe cracker?" He resumed his search underneath his bed.

"What are you doing?"

"My car keys are attached to the same ring."

"Ahh." I climbed into bed.

"My car's fast. I'm a professional driver. We'll make a hell of a getaway."

"Right." I looked forward to breakfast, lunch, and dinner. I looked forward to seeing Kathleen. I looked forward to whatever phone calls I would receive. I was already tired.

I rolled onto my side and waited for tomorrow.

35

ACTING-DRIVER

WE HAD AN OLD fill-in piece in place of our regular engine, which had to go to the city's Master Mechanic's Shop for repair while C-shift was on duty. Our regular driver, Sam, had to take leave or lose it; we were allowed to carry four hundred and ninety hours on the books. I was up for acting-driver, since Ric drove last.

Also, since Ric had the night-trick off, the captain preferred to have the acting-driver remain on the piece for a twenty-four-hour shift, if possible. Acting-drivers, by definition, were not as skillful as the regular driver and were not as knowledgeable of the streets. And if the acting-driver hasn't been behind the wheel for a while, then it takes a trip to the store and a couple of minor runs to bring the acting-driver's confidence up to a comfortable level. Once that level has been achieved, most captains are reluctant to relinquish it to another acting-driver, especially during a night-trick when the sudden disorientation of the alarm's arousal increases the burden on the acting man.

Larry Gorden, from Station Thirteen, was the tailboard fill-in man replacing our rookie, T. C., who had been sent to Rescue Nine for the day-trick to employ his shock trauma skills. Larry was a veteran fire fighter with twenty years, and he was a longtime friend of mine. We shared a few minutes talking old times in the galley, over morning coffee, then I tore myself away from the shift-change gathering to familiarize myself with the engine.

With my second cup of coffee in hand, I stood in front of the pump panel and studied the gauges and knobs, as well as the numbered levers that corresponded with the numbered hoselines, to an engine I had not driven in many years. I recognized the piece as old Engine Ten.

The apparatus was worn out and had no business being on line, even as a backup piece. But the department was always under-budgeted and was forced to use old equipment until it was finally replaced forever.

I set my coffee cup on the engine's sideboard below the pump panel and climbed up into the basket. I opened the fill opening to make sure the water tank was full; I didn't trust the gauges on this old war horse.

While I was up there, I checked the hose lays on the rear and cross-lay hosebeds in front. The five-inch looked fine and the two-and-a-half was packed on the left rear bed. Since the two-and-a-half was not preconnected, it had to be broken off and connected to one of the discharge outlets on either side of the engine. There were two sets of inch-and-three-quarter lines in the cross-lay beds that were four sections long, and there was an inch-and-three-quarters line in the right rear bed that was six sections long.

I scanned the basket to see what tools it contained, then climbed down the side of the engine to drink more coffee and study the pump panel layout again.

I double-checked which preconnected line went with what discharge valve, played with the pressure gauge, located my fill valve and fill line, and generally made sure I knew which valve went with each discharge outlet and intake. I opened the engineer's compartment next to the pump panel and made sure I had a rubber mallet, the various size spanner wrenches, the various types and sizes of couplings, wyes, and gates, as well as the full array of tools that I required.

I set my coffee cup back on the sideboard, climbed into the cab, and turned on the battery. The gauge arrows on the dashboard jumped lively to their readings and the radio squawked. I checked the fuel and oil and air pressure readings, and noted the five-speed manual transmission gearshift diagram. Then I located the pump gear knob and the parking air brakes and the emergency running lights master switch, which I decided to turn on. I jumped out of the cab and made sure all the rotating and flashing emergency lights were operating.

I felt fairly confident when I climbed back into the cab to turn off the running lights. I was planning to start the engine and place it into pump gear, to make sure the engine was capable of providing water and to make sure I knew what I was doing, when the brass hit.

"Ten-one house fire. Engine Fifteen, respond to 1137 Virgilina Avenue on a ten-one house fire. Flames and smoke visible. Victims trapped on the second floor. Time out: 0650."

I ran to the large wall map on the apparatus floor to pinpoint the location of the house. As soon as I found the eleven-hundred block of Virgilina, I oriented myself, by locating our station on the map, and chose my route to the scene.

Left on Fishermans Road, right on Sturgis Road, right on Sturgis Street, then left on Virgilina, and—no, wait—I noticed an unfamiliar line drawn on the map that seemed to indicate a median that split the thirteen-hundred block of Virgilina Road. I was afraid I might have to go around this obstruction and lose time.

I altered my route and decided to take a left on Modoc Avenue from Sturgis Street, then a right on Warwick Avenue, and a left on Virgilina. Since there were trapped victims, we were on rescue mode and, therefore, I wasn't concerned about catching a hydrant.

I knew the captain would make sure Thirteen Engine would bring one in.

I ran to the cab, climbed onboard, started the piece, and waited for the tailboard men to step into their turnout pants and fire boots and climb into their open jump seats.

The captain keyed his portable radio. "Engine Fifteen's responding." Then he climbed onboard with his turnout gear already on. "Do you know where you're going?"

"I've got it," I said.

"Good."

Ric slapped the window behind me twice, signaling me to go, as well as indicating that everybody was safely onboard.

One slap meant stop. Two slaps meant go. Three slaps meant reverse. These were the standard signals used in the fire service, especially in the recent past—before every fire fighter carried a portable radio. On ladder trucks, electrical buzzers were used to send these signals between the driver and the tillerman. On life lines, hand pulls were used as the method of signaling between the inside rescuing fire fighter and the outside tender. On an old fire engine like this, where the cab was separated from the open air jump seats, which also faced the opposite direction of travel, hand slaps were used against the rear cab's window or on top of the engine's housing to communicate to the driver and the captain.

As soon as I drove onto Fishermans Road, the captain turned on the siren, then opened the map book to verify the location of the address and check the whereabouts of a hydrant. Ric and Larry were struggling into their turnout coats, as well as into the straps of their tank harnesses; I heard the bells to their tanks ring, indicating that they had turned on their air.

"Battalion Two, Engine Fifteen."

"Engine Fifteen."

"Conduct a rescue for probable trapped victims upon arrival."

"Ten-four." Ron slid open the window behind him to communicate with the fire fighter sitting in the open jump seat. "Larry!"

"Yeah, Captain!?"

"Go in for a rescue as soon as we arrive!"

"Right!"

"Tell Ric to follow you in with a line!"

"Right!"

"Larry!"

"What!?"

"Tell Ric I'm his backup!"

"Okay!"

The captain slid the window closed to reduce the diesel engine's noise that roared from underneath the engine's housing that separated the two jump seats; he began buttoning down and tanking up. "I think we've got something, Danny."

My eyes never left the road. "I think you're right." By this time, we were traveling on Modoc and heading for Warwick.

I grew calm, despite my unfamiliarity with the piece or my general inexperience with driving. When I reached Warwick, I downshifted into second gear from fourth, since the constant approach of side-street intersections prevented me from safely going into fifth, and made a hard right. I glanced into my left side mirror, as I came out of the turn, and saw my coffee cup sail into the air and shatter on the street.

I smelled smoke. Virgilina was three streets away. When I made the final left, I saw fire on both floors of the house.

The captain keyed his radio. "Engine Fifteen's on the scene. We have a fully involved, two-story brick structure with smoke and flames visible on both floors. Engine Fifteen is in the rescue mode. Engine Fifteen's in command."

"Ten-four, Engine Fifteen."

"Engine Fifteen to Engine Thirteen."

"Engine Thirteen, go ahead."

"We're goin' to need that hydrant."

"Ten-four."

"Engine Fifteen, Ladder Thirteen."

"Ladder Thirteen, go ahead."

"Ladder the second floor for rescue."

"Ten-four."

The house was on my side. I stopped the engine in front of the house, which had a sizable front yard, then shifted into neutral and set the parking brakes. The captain climbed out of the cab as Larry hustled to the house with a set of irons. Ric maneuvered to the side hosebed, grabbed the nozzle along with part of the six-section line, and headed for the front door as I pushed in on the clutch, shifted into fourth gear, reached down and turned the pump gear knob, then released the clutch slowly to engage the pump gear. I felt the change in the engine's idle and verified this changing into pump gear by checking the RPMs on my tachometer.

"Battalion Two is on the scene."

"Ten-four, Battalion Two."

"Battalion Two is in command."

"Ten-four."

I climbed out of the cab and went to the pump panel where I pulled the lever out to drop the tank. Then I pulled the rest of the hose out of the bed as Ric and Ron dragged the line toward the front door.

Larry pried the front door open by using a halligan tool and flat head axe, donned his facepiece, and went inside while Ric and Ron brought the nozzle to the door. As I pulled the valve to charge the line, Ric followed Larry inside and Ron cracked open the nozzle to bleed the line and adjust the setting. Then I cranked up the pressure to a hundred psi to make sure there was enough water pressure, as Ron went inside with the line.

I heard Thirteen Engine coming to me.

I opened the engineer's compartment, took out the rubber mallet, and smacked it hard against the upper wing of the five-inch cap to loosen it up so I could unscrew the cap from the main intake butterfly valve. Once I had the cap off, I released the five-inch intake adaptor from its side mount and attached it to the butterfly flow control device. Then I unbuckled the five-inch flexible hose from the leather straps on both ends, pulled it off the storage rail that ran the length of the engine's side, and attached it to the other end of the five-inch intake adaptor.

I heard screaming children.

Crow, the Thirteen Engine's driver, and Elly, a fire fighter, dragged the broken-off five-inch to the end of my five-inch hookup line and coupled them with a set of spanner wrenches they brought with them. A moment later, Crow hollered, "Your five-inch is connected!"

I ran to the cab and pulled the lanyard to my air horn hard and long to tell the hydrant man to give me water. Then I reached for my portable radio. "Engine Fifteen to the hydrant."

"Water's coming to you, Engine Fifteen."

"Ten-four."

I heard children screaming. I heard Larry crying.

I hopped out of the cab and went back to the pump panel to make sure the bleeder valve was open on the five-inch intake adaptor. Engine Company Thirteen was already laying the other inch-and-three-quarters line off the engine's side hosebed toward the house. When the five-inch flexible hose began to tighten, I opened the five-inch intake butterfly valve to receive the hydrant's water and closed the bleeder valve. As soon as the boys from Engine Thirteen had the line at the door, I charged it and adjusted the pressure. I was watching my gauges, prepared for a sudden drop in pressure, when they opened up this second line.

As I stood by my pump panel, I noticed that Ladder Thirteen was parked in the opposite direction, facing my engine, and was engaged in laddering one of the windows on the second floor. Then I saw Engine Sixteen bringing in their own hydrant. The Sixteen Engine boys grabbed a line off their piece and dragged it to the back of the house while their driver prepared his pump to give them water, as well as prepared his pump to receive water from the second hydrant.

"Crow!" I hollered. "Help him hook up his five-inch! I'm doing fine!"

"Right!" Crow hurried to LeGrand and gave him a hand.

The psi drop on my gauges indicated that Engine Company Thirteen had opened up the second line inside to back up Fifteen's attack/rescue line against the heavy fire; I raised the pressure.

Suddenly, Larry stumbled out of the blackness of the front door and fell to his knees. He tossed back his helmet and ripped off his facemask and began sobbing. "I couldn't get to them! I couldn't get to them!"

I wanted to go to him, but I was afraid to abandon my engine's pump panel. I saw Wyatt, who was on Rescue Thirteen. "Wyatt! Something's wrong with Larry!" I pointed at Larry for emphasis. "Over there! Over there!"

Wyatt ran to Larry and knelt beside him. Several other fire fighters converged on him as well.

"The children!" Larry cried. "I couldn't reach them! Too hot! Too hot! I couldn't save them!" Larry bent forward, supported by his hands, and cried convulsively.

The fire had spread throughout the house before the alarm was sent. By the time we arrived on the scene, the parents were already asphyxiated by smoke and the children were already beyond rescue; they were burning alive as Larry tried to reach them.

I slumped against the pump panel and quietly shook my head. If Sam hadn't been forced to take leave, I would have been the one standing in the wrong place at the wrong time; I would have been the recipient of an unwarranted guilt for the rest of my life.

They sent Larry home, classified with an in-line-of-duty injury, and replaced him with a hireback. And the children, like their parents, died of asphyxiation.

I hoped Larry had a sympathetic wife.

36

TAILBOARD FIRE FIGHTER

"You'll live a long time with medications, and if you take care of yourself." Dr. Guttimann seemed positive, yet I detected a grave undertone in his voice.

They had taken me to a private room for recovery, where I had to remain flat on my back and immobile for twelve hours. My right leg had been secured to the bed with a folded bedsheet laid across my thigh and tucked under both sides of the mattress.

Kathleen was standing at my bedside, visibly relieved. I reached for her forearm with my right hand.

"Okay, Doc," I said, "I'll live a long time. But I feel awful. Is that going to go away?"

"We have medications that will hopefully manage your coronary vasospasms to some degree."

"You also said I had a small blockage when you were doing the catheterization."

"Minor. That blockage is minor."

"A coronary . . . ."

"Artery spasm."

"Is it permanent?"

The doctor smiled to foster optimism. "Yes. But we can manage that, along with your hypertension and angina, with medication—we hope."

"See? You're going to be alright," Kathleen said.

I smiled at her to reflect the doctor's optimism. I patted her forearm. She reached for my hand and held it.

"Is my blood pressure under control?"

"No. But try not to worry. These things take time."

"I see." I sighed. "I've told you this already, Doc. But . . . but inside of me, it . . . it feels as if a switch has been turned off inside of me. I feel weak and washed out all the time. I have no energy or stamina or strength. Will these things come back to me?"

"Ahh, yes, well—"

"Come on, Doc, don't hold back. When can I get out of here?"

I'd given him a means to avoid my initial question. He seized the opportunity.

"Tomorrow. I'll have you out of here by tomorrow." Dr. Guttimann began to leave. "I'll be back this afternoon to check in on you."

"Wait a minute, Doc." His attitude deflated and revealed a hint of impatience.

"The doctor has to go, honey. He has other patients."

"I know, honey, I know." I smiled at her to suppress my impatience with the doctor. "Just one more question, Doc."

"Sure."

I looked straight into his eyes. "I can go home tomorrow, but when can I go back to work?"

Dr. Guttimann averted his eyes. "Yes, well, you see—"

"In plain language, Doctor Guttimann."

"Your cardio architecture is shot." He finally looked at me. "You're done fire fighting."

The declaration stunned me. I looked at my wife, who seemed relieved by the news.

"But, Doc, I love my job. You've got to give me a clean bill of health. I'm a tailboard fire fighter. It's what I do."

"If I send you back to this . . . this so-called tailboard, you're going to die on that tailboard."

I deflated. "Whoa."

"You can live a long life," he added. "But not as a fire fighter. The stress would be too much for you. In fact, the stress and demands of your job are the obvious cause of your present heart condition." He clasped his hands together. "Look. You survived one heart attack on the job. You may not survive another. You must avoid stress." He unclasped his hands and shrugged his shoulders. "You're done. I'm sorry. I'll be back this afternoon."

"Okay, Doc. Okay."

Kathleen and I were silent for a long time.

"Are you alright?" she said.

"What's alright?"

"I don't mind telling you—"

"I know, I know—"

"You can't know how much I've worried about you all these years."

"I've never told you anything about my work."

"That's a good thing. I wouldn't have let you stay with the fire department otherwise."

"Don't be ridiculous," I said, irritably.

"It was bad enough getting those phone calls through the years—"

"What calls?"

"The ones informing me that you were in the hospital with an injury. Don't worry, they would say, he's alright. He's alright. But I wasn't alright."

"They were minor injuries."

"Not at ten o'clock at night over the telephone. They weren't minor to me."

Silence allowed the tension between us to dissipate.

"I love you, Danny. And I'm sorry. But I won't miss your being a fire fighter. I'm glad. I'm relieved. I'm sorry."

I took her hand in mine. "No. I'm sorry. This job of mine has put you through a lot. I love you, Kathleen."

"I learned to live with your job. You were happy. You never complained about the work or the hours or the administration. But now that it's over, well—I'm relieved." She squeezed my hand. "You're alive. And you're mine."

"I turned my head away from her and looked out the window. "Yeah."

She stirred. "Are you alright?"

I hesitated. "Yeah." But I wasn't. And I wouldn't be for a long time. I knew that. My cowboy days were over and I was facing the prospects of an ordinary life.

I gently squeezed my wife's hand and closed my eyes and let her loving presence soften the impact of this terrible news.

She let me have the silence I required, because she believed I was fundamentally tough and resilient. She believed I'd find a way to face this forced change in my life.

I squeezed her hand and closed my eyes. Anyway, that's what I believed she believed. And that's what I hoped.

ANKLE DEEP IN WATER

Askewed watercolors
smudged and cracked and
nameless with damage;
hanging in a long hallway
in a burned out structure;
from the blaze a kind of death
face to face on both walls:
landscapes and seascapes
unnoticed losses by firemen
ankle deep in water,
soot covered and tired from the battle . . .
overlooked decor by their owner
their existence forgotten,
astonished and exhausted by the spectacle
of destruction.

Upon one thing
my loneliness is amplified,
my sadness is focused
upon its broken beauty,
upon its last surviving moment
briefly captured by my hushed silence,
my admiration,
my appreciation, while standing
before the remains of,
a "still life."

AUTHOR'S BIOGRAPHY

D.S. LLITERAS is the author of ten books that have received national and international acclaim. Some of his novels have been translated into Italian, Russian, and Japanese. His short stories and poetry have appeared in numerous national and international magazines, journals, and anthologies.

D.S. Lliteras enlisted in the U.S. Navy after high school and served in Vietnam as a combat corpsman attached to the First Reconnaissance Battalion, First Marine Division, earning a Bronze Star Medal (with Combat "V"). While in country, Lliteras completed twenty long range reconnaissance patrols and eighty combat dives.

After his discharge in 1970, he enrolled at Florida State University where he received his Bachelor of Arts and Master of Fine Arts degrees.

Lliteras worked as a theatrical director until 1979 then quit directing and became a merchant sailor. In 1981, he earned a commission in the U.S. Navy and served as a Deep Sea Diving and Salvage Officer. After several years of service, which included extreme, arduous sea duty, Lliteras resigned his naval commission and became a professional fire fighter.

After retiring from the fire department, he has been able to devote his full time to writing fiction.

PRAISE FOR THE WORK OF D. S. LLITERAS

"Lliteras is a powerful writer who can wring emotions out of a stone."
—*Affaire de Coeur*

"Easily one of the best authors of biblical fiction today."
—*Library Journal*, 02/01/07

"Lliteras' brand of biblical fiction is heart-racing; it's messy, bloody and honest."
—*Publishers Weekly*

"*The Silence of John* is a fabulous entry in a terrific and insightful series."
—*Midwest Book Review*

"*613 West Jefferson*, by D.S. Lliteras, is a fine example of a book that tells a story where Vietnam is both everywhere and nowhere at the same time. There's drama. There's action. There's an interesting and unusual story. But most important, there's truth. And there's also some magic."
—*VietNow*

"With just six words, he pens profundity: 'between space and time . . . infinity arises.'"
—*The Virginian-Pilot*

"Lliteras' genius is wide-ranging. He is not only a unique stylist, but a great storyteller as well."
—*New Age Retailer*

"Lliteras takes on life's biggest issues. This is not an easy task, but he handles it very well."
—*The VVA*

"D.S. Lliteras listens to the human heartbeat with an utterly sincere, spiritual stethoscope, and every line he writes aches and sweats and breathes with the endless noble toil of human flesh. *In the Heart of Things* gets my vote as the most human novel of 1992."
—Gerald Nicosia, author of *Memory Babe: A Critical Biography of Jack Kerouac*

"To his credit, Mr. Lliteras experiments with literary structure, using a Pinteresque play-within-a-play and poetry to reflect his character's metaphysical struggle and awareness."
—*The Baltimore Sun*

"Lliteras has a rugged Ernest Hemingway background but a sensitive Emily Dickinson message: 'Walk invisibly in the world; escape into life.'"
—*The Virginian-Pilot*

"You don't read this book. With a slight touch of embarrassment you look over Lliteras' shoulder and gently finger the old photograph on one side of the page and then linger over his thoughts that are printed on the other side . . . This is a very fine book, as much for what it doesn't do as for what it does. Few books that make it to the book counter are so devoid of pretension and bombast, especially when it comes to all the first hand accounts about Vietnam."
—*Vietnam Magazine*

"Through a searching for the meaning of life and death . . . this book lays bare the innermost thoughts of a man on a journey."
—*The Paperback Forum*

RELATED TITLES

If you enjoyed *Flames and Smoke Visible*, you may also enjoy other Rainbow Ridge titles. Read more about them at *www.rainbowridgebooks.com*

The Cosmic Internet: Explanations from the Other Side
by Frank DeMarco

Difficult People: A Gateway to Enlightenment
by Lisette Larkins

Dance of the Electric Hummingbird
by Patricia Walker

Coming Full Circle: Ancient Teachings for a Modern World
by Lynn Andrews

Thank Your Wicked Parents
by Richard Bach

Consciousness: Bridging the Gap Between Conventional Science and the New Super Science of Quantum Mechanics
by Eva Herr

Blue Sky, White Clouds
by Eliezer Sobel

Rainbow Ridge Books publishes spiritual and metaphysical titles, and is distributed by Square One Publishers in Garden City Park, New York.

To contact authors and editors, peruse our titles, and see submission guidelines, please visit our website at *www.rainbowridgebooks.com*.

For orders and catalogs, please call toll-free: (877) 900-BOOK.